The Weight of Silence

Invisible Children of India

Shelley Seale

DEV
Dog's Eye View Media
Hot Springs, South Dakota USA

Published in the United States by Dog's Eye View Media
www.DogsEyeViewMedia.com

ISBN: 978-0-9802323-7-0

LCCN: 2009928185

Edited by Barbara Hautanen

Design by Nola Lee Kelsey

Cover photo by Craig A. Lakey

Note: The names of some of the children have been changed to protect their identities.

Dedicated to -

The incredible, beautiful children of India

Contents

"Our lives begin to end the day we become silent about things that matter."

–Dr. Martin Luther King, Jr.

Foreword by Joan Collins

Even though I have never been to India, I have supported many children from there for the past several decades. I knew little about the difficulties that so many children on that continent have to live with but was glad to know that my support to The Christian Children's Fund helped these children have adequate food, housing and schooling. My tiny monthly stipend seemed to go far, as often I'd receive letters of grateful thanks from some of the children who were able to finish school and even attend college.

My charitable efforts have always been on behalf of children, whether it be the NSPCC, The International Foundation for Children with Learning Disabilities, the Children's Hospital of Michigan, Caudwell Children or my own charity - the Shooting Star Hospice. I feel that children are the most vulnerable to abuse and hardship and therefore the most needy of our protection and help.

Shelley Seale's life-affirming and sensitive book brings into sharp focus the millions of children whose lives have been blighted by poverty, disease, abuse and more than anything the lack of parents or caregivers. India is continuing to become more prosperous yet there are nearly 25 million children (yes, *million*) growing up on the streets, in orphanages and without any kind of family of their own. Two million a year die from the kind of diseases that have been eradicated in the West or are treatable: Malaria, TB, Polio and Tetanus are preventable and with proper medication these kids would not have to die.

And of course there is AIDS. India has the largest HIV population in the world, and it has created a massive orphan rate. India has little money to fund HIV treatment so the statistic is supposed to double in five years time. One of every three malnourished children live in India and 50% of deaths are due to malnutrition and starvation.

Child trafficking and prostitution, as well as child slave labor, are other terrible problems. India accounts for 40% of the world's child trafficking, and there are half a million child prostitutes in India, euphemistically described as "sex workers." And as the movie "Slumdog Millionaire" so painfully portrayed, thousands of helpless children are deliberately maimed and sent out on the streets to beg, not for themselves but for the brutal mafia-style gangs that exploit them.

There are no human rights for any of these children, and so Shelley became involved with The Miracle Foundation, which supports children in India's orphanages.

In her journeys through the slums, streets and clinics of India, she has chronicled the children's hopes and hardships and their ability to overcome crippling challenges. It is truly inspirational.

One of the greatest tragedies for these poor forgotten children is that the majority of citizens ignore them. As they sleep in the streets, bus shelters or train stations, people do not care. They just step over them as if they do not exist.

I hope this book will cast light on the immense human tragedy and that the world will no longer ignore these precious children.

Joan Collins, January 2009 Joan Collins is first and foremost an actress, but she is also a best-selling author, accomplished producer, a successful entrepreneur and a devoted mother. She is deeply concerned about children the world over and is an honorary founding member of the National Society for the Prevention of Cruelty to Children. She has supported several foster children in India for 25 years. She is a patron of The Shooting Star Hospice, which opened its doors to terminally ill children and their families, thanks in part to fundraising efforts led by Joan. In 1997 Her Majesty Queen Elizabeth II presented Joan Collins with the Most Excellent Order of the British Empire (O.B.E.) for her lifetime contribution to the arts and her continuing charity work.

Introduction: Silent Disasters

There is a holocaust quietly happening among India's children. The perpetrator is poverty, and its foot soldiers are disease, gender and caste discrimination, unclean water, illiteracy, and malnutrition. Its allies are corruption, ineffective government policies, and rich industrialized nations that, in an indifferent and arrogant imbalance of global power, claim exemption from a battle fought on such far lands. While there may be no Adolf Hitler or Idi Amin behind it, make no mistake – it is a holocaust all the same.

While this silent war is waged against millions of children, a very different India is the one we see and hear about. Its emergence on the international markets with leading industries such as technology, pharmaceuticals and manufacturing have put it squarely in the center of global importance, with an astounding annual growth rate of nine percent bringing an influx of new wealth daily. The country

is home to the fastest-growing middle class in history;
whose numbers, at over three hundred million, are more
than the entire population of the United States.[i] India has
emerged as one of the world's greatest wealth creators,
thanks to a buoyant stock market and high earnings.[ii]
Stories about this shimmering new India fill newspapers
and business magazines.

Yet amidst this growing prosperity there is a hidden
India. Hundreds of millions are excluded from the boom,
living completely outside the affluence it brings. They exist
on its periphery, pushed to the margins, and often seem a
source of embarrassment to those who wish to present only
the shiny new face of Indian success. In this other India an
entire generation of parentless children is growing up –
more than twenty-five million of them,[iii] with close to four
million more joining their ranks each year.[iv] India is also
home to the most AIDS orphans of any country in the
world, approaching two million – a number that is expected
to double over the next five years.[v]

The effect that the growing epidemic will have on
children is scarcely comprehensible in a country where far
too many are already orphaned by treatable diseases such
as malaria, tuberculosis, worms, even simple diarrhea. More
than two million children themselves die every year from
preventable infections for which education and medicine
are lacking.[vi] One of every three of the world's
malnourished children lives in India, and about fifty
percent of childhood deaths there are attributable to
malnutrition or starvation.[vii] Many of India's children are, in

fact, orphaned due to poverty rather than death; their families are simply too poor to feed them. Their plights go virtually unnoticed by the world, their voices silenced. They are invisible children, a generation being denied its rights, hopes, and aspirations. These are the silent disasters.

I first went to India as a volunteer, to work and play with a group of children living in a small orphanage. These beautiful children had all been affected by one or more of these issues; and as I bore witness to the harm that lay in each of them because of it, as I discovered the stories behind the faces and the names, there was simply no way to go on with my life afterwards as if they did not exist. And so I embarked on a three-year venture that took me all across the country and into hundreds of children's lives, through hours upon hours of research and interviews with social workers, doctors, orphanage directors, government officials and humanitarians. My sole purpose was to give these millions of children a voice that could be heard by others in the world who, I was convinced, would be as moved by their plights as I was.

In my journeys over the last years into the orphanages, slums, clinics and streets of India I have become immersed in the world of these children. Their hope and resilience amazed me time and time again; the ability of their spirits to overcome crippling challenges inspired me. Even in the most deprived circumstances they are still kids – they laugh and play, perhaps far less frequently than others; they develop strong bonds and relationships to create family where none exists; and most of all they have an enormous amount of love to give.

The stories told in this book do not belong to me. They were given to me as a gift, often because I was the only person who had ever asked. And so I am merely the narrator who attempts to relay their stories to others, for that is the only thing I have to offer.

I want to be clear that although this book deals with struggles and failures, this is far from the only side of India. The country is an astonishing place full of history, grand architecture, magnificent natural beauty and some of the most wonderful people I have ever met. Because this book focuses on those excluded from the riches of their nation, the topics and issues written about often show a darker side of India. Yet during my journeys and research the other, beautiful India constantly showed itself, even in the most difficult places. It is an extraordinarily wonderful place and I encourage anyone who has the chance to visit.

I also want to state up front that the aim of this book is not for westerners, such as myself, to tell Indians how they should solve their problems. Our culture has plenty of our own on which to focus. Most of the western world's knowledge of India's shortcomings is derived from western media and foreign development agencies, whose goal is often to please donors or people in power – in a word, outsiders. Not Indians themselves. Us outsiders, the humanitarian agencies and foreign aid programs, will always fall short in one important way. We do not and cannot know what is best for India. It is not a matter for us

to come and instruct or order; for efforts undertaken in that
way, no matter how well intentioned, will always fail in
their arrogance. Foreigners rarely fully understand the
society they think to "improve," and the potential for
imposing their own cultural bias can result in negative
consequences for those whose lives they seek to change. We
should come to listen, to learn, to assist where and when
asked; and so the goal of this book is simply to allow us to
hear what those voices have to say.

Many people ask me, why India? And my simple
answer is, why not? I find most people who ask this
question are really asking, why don't you do something
here at home instead of traveling halfway around the
world? There are plenty of children here who are suffering
and need help. I agree, and donate significant amounts of
both time and money to nonprofits doing incredible work
for children right here in the United States.

But besides that, why India? Because I believe that
every life, no matter where it's lived, has equal value.
Because extreme poverty in India is not the same as poverty
in the United States. Because there are very little if any
safety nets for these children who fall through the cracks.
Although we have vast problems in my home country as
well, millions of children in the U.S. aren't generally
threatened by malaria and tuberculosis, denied their entire
educations or trafficked, sold into factories or domestic
labor if they're lucky, to brothels if they're not. A childhood
cannot wait for the AIDS epidemic to subside, for poverty
to be eradicated, for adults and governments to act, for the

world to notice them. Once gone, their childhoods can never be regained.

And quite simply, because those twenty-five million children exist.

_i_ Outlook India, "Elephant Must Remember" by Alam Srinivas, April 9, 2007.

_ii_ Indian Economy: An Overview, Nov 13 2006.

iii The Joint United Nations Programme on HIV/AIDS (UNAIDS), the United Nations Children's Fund (UNICEF), and the United States Agency for International Development (USAID), <u>Children on the Brink 2004: A Joint Report of New Orphan Estimates and a Framework for Action</u>, July 2004.

_v_ World Bank, <u>At-A-Glance India: AIDS and Orphans</u>.

_vi_ USAID website, India Country Profile, http://www.usaid.gov/policy/budget/cbj2005/ane/in.html.

vii UNICEF website, "India – Children's Issues: Early Years," http://www.unicef.org/india/children_140.htm.

"India was the mother of our race and Sanskrit the mother of Europe's languages. She was the mother of our philosophy, mother through the Arabs, of much of our mathematics, mother through Buddha, of the ideals embodied in Christianity, mother through village communities of self-government and democracy. Mother India is in many ways the mother of us all."

–*Will Durant*

Surrounded by Children

March 12, 2006

Lurching along the dirt road, I gaze out the window at rural Orissa in northeastern India as the car bounces over potholes sending plumes of red dust billowing behind it. The small villages we pass are as familiar to me as if I had been here only last week. Shacks line the river, their plastic or tar paper roofs held down with rocks. The smell of curry and incense hangs thick in the air. The tiny shops and vendor stalls selling saris or pots or candies, the mangy dogs and cows nosing at piles of trash, the rickshaw drivers pedaling through traffic alongside schoolgirls with their braided hair and backpacks; people seem to fill every square inch of space. It is exactly as I left it a year ago.

I glance at my daughter, Chandler, sitting next to me, trying to gauge her feelings. She's looking out the far window with eager eyes. It's not the street life we're passing that has Chandler enthralled. Although it's her first trip to India, we have been traveling in the country for over a week now and she's grown familiar with the scene outside the window. Like me, she is excited to be on our way to the orphanage, at last. It is the reason we are here in the first place; the reason I have brought my fifteen year old child halfway around the world. We will spend a week at the Miracle Foundation home with a hundred children who had captured my heart the year before. Their photographs line the walls of my house. Occasional letters and drawings arrive from them. I write about them and fundraise for them. My desire to bring my own daughter to this place, this experience, has led us to this moment.

I turn my head back toward the passing palm and ashoka trees, and the river glittering in the afternoon sun. Questions ricochet silently inside me. What will the kids look like? Will they have changed? Will they remember me? What will Chandler's reaction be? Suddenly we are pulling through the gates into the ashram. The large open space in the middle of the compound is empty, no one there to greet us. I realize they are not yet expecting us. We get out of the car and start up the little pathway that leads between buildings to the interior courtyard.

One by one, they begin to spy us. I see little brown faces peeking out around corners and through bushes. Slowly the ashram comes to life. Word of our arrival spreads and dozens of grinning, jumping children surround us on the path and pour into the courtyard. Within seconds, we are engulfed by barefoot children grasping for our hands and clambering over each other, smiling up at us. Ten feet away, yet separated by twenty bodies bouncing between us, Chandler stands with several kids holding each hand and more clinging to her arms. Her pale skin and long blonde hair are almost lost in the sea of them. She knows many on sight, familiar with their stories and the pictures she's seen countless times. The amazement on her face makes her look even younger than her fifteen years.

"Hello," "Welcome," "Good Evening," the children say. Small hands reach for me. There's Santosh! And Sibani, Daina, Salu . . . I pick up the tiny ones like Papuni and search for other faces I haven't seen yet. Children run up to show me small things I had given them the year before – stickers, crayons, hair clips. They display these cherished treasures; such simple possessions, so proudly owned and taken care of. They ask for nothing from me other than being here. In many ways they are just like other children I've known with homes and families of their own – except for their neediness, their raw hunger for affection, love, belonging.

They had been imprinted on my soul forever.

* * *

I never expected to be in India. And without a doubt, I never thought once I had been I would return, again and again.

It wasn't the exotic beauty that drew me back. It wasn't the warmth of the people, their gentle and inquisitive nature, their open hospitality. It wasn't the storied, ancient

history of the country or its rich and varied culture. It was
not the colors or the spices or the sounds or the spirituality
of the place. India is all of these things, to be sure, and I
have grown to love them all. But they were not what seeped
into my being and pulled me close, becoming a part of me
that I missed with a strange emptiness when I left.

It was the children.

They are everywhere. They fill the railway stations, the
cities, the shanty villages. Some scrounge through trash for
newspapers, rags or anything they can sell at traffic
intersections. Others, often as young as two or three years
old, beg. Many are homeless, overflowing the orphanages
and other institutional homes to live on the streets. I had no
way of knowing just how much they would change my life.

As the New Year dawned on 2004 I was living in
Austin, Texas, freelancing and trying to single-handedly
shepherd a thirteen-year-old daughter through her teenage
years unscathed. I felt slightly adrift after recently leaving
Dallas, a relationship and a full-time real estate business to
craft a life with more meaning. For me this meant going
back to school, embracing my first passion of writing
instead of the career I had haphazardly fallen into, and
engaging myself more deeply with social and political
issues of importance to me.

I had always been involved in children's rights and
nonprofit work with youth – mentoring at-risk teen girls,
volunteering with Child Protective Services, and standing
up for children as a court-appointed advocate when they
had been removed from parents due to abuse or neglect.

This interest had been sparked in me early when my mother became a foster parent at a home for unwed mothers. More than fifty babies lived with us over the years on their journeys to adoptive families. In 1984 my own parents adopted my youngest sister just as I was graduating from high school.

One day in early 2004, I was paging through a local lifestyle magazine, Tribeza, when an article grabbed my attention. It told the story of Caroline Boudreaux, who had visited India three years earlier and happened upon a home full of parentless children living in incomprehensible conditions. That night a toddler named Sibani walked over and laid her head on Caroline's knee. Caroline picked her up and rocked her to sleep, singing a lullaby as Sibani pressed her small body into Caroline's. When Sibani was asleep Caroline carried her to bed, but what she found chilled her. The room was filled with thirty wooden frameworks that looked like picnic tables; no mattresses, no pillows, no blankets. The couple who ran the orphanage constantly lacked enough food, clothing and supplies to adequately provide for the children they had taken in - children who had nowhere else to turn. Caroline had to put the sleeping baby down on the hard slat that served as her crib, hearing her bones clack against the wood.

The moment she returned to the United States, Caroline left her career in television advertising behind and started a nonprofit organization to raise funds for the children in the home, in spite of having no idea what she was doing or how to do it. She simply knew she had to do something. Next to the article was a full-page photograph of Caroline Boudreaux holding a picture of the little girl, Sibani, who had so altered her life's path.

I wondered what could be so powerful about these kids that they would cause a person to completely turn her life upside down. And what kind of a woman *does* that? I decided this was a woman that I wanted to know. That afternoon I sent an email to Caroline, telling her I'd like to learn more about the work she was doing and if there were ways I could help. She replied the next day, and the following week I was sitting in her living room with a handful of other supporters.

"Hey, girl! It's good to meet you, thanks for coming," Caroline welcomed me in an easy, friendly manner with her Louisiana Cajun drawl and infectious laugh. She offered pizza and wine, brushing back rebellious pieces of her curly dark hair that escaped from the barrette attempting to tame it. As she spoke to the small group about the children and her fledgling organization's needs, Caroline's eyes were serious and the strength and passion of her dedication evident.

I walked away from that evening committed to redesigning and producing The Miracle Foundation's newsletter and volunteering at the next fundraising event. For the first time in my life there were thoughts of India in my head.

* * *

As I became more involved with the foundation, the friendship between Caroline and I grew. Her vivacious personality and enthusiasm drew people to her cause, but she was far from a meek, demure saint-like figure. Her blunt outspokenness and irreverent sense of humor endeared her to me as a person – a real person who was on as much a mission for her own fulfillment as a selfless Mother Theresa-style mission of mercy. This was no charity Caroline Boudreaux was running. She wasn't asking people to give a handout for poor little third world orphans because they felt sorry for them. She was demanding that the world take notice of them and their inherent rights.

"We're a rights organization," she told me. "We're not here because these kids are poor, or Indian, or untouchables. We're here to ensure the rights they have by birth: food, clean water, a home, medical care, an education. The right to the most basic of things: a childhood."

Her words resonated in me. It seemed a somewhat novel approach compared to the familiar "flies on sad children's faces" commercials. Caroline's goal wasn't sympathy, motivating people by making these kids pitiful enough to pull on the heartstrings, but rather by the simple fact that they are our future and deserve the basic necessities in life – by right, not by benevolence. Other people had the ability to ensure those rights for them. It was a simple calculable solution, in fact a moral imperative.

By that fall I had pitched her story to a local magazine I wrote for and was given the assignment. I met Caroline at Starbucks to interview her formally for the article. The first question I asked was how she'd had the courage to leave her job and entire lifestyle behind on what must have seemed like an impractical whim at the time.

"I hated that life," she admitted. After eight years in the television business she was restless, burned out of the job and the corporate scene. "I felt there must be more to life, but I had no idea what else I might do."

The stress became too much one morning, driving to work in heavy traffic with a cup of coffee between her knees and an irate client on the cell phone. "I just snapped," Caroline said. "I couldn't take it anymore. I knew this was not what I wanted."

The trouble was she didn't know what she *did* want to do with her life. She and a friend decided to quit their jobs and travel the globe. With a huge world map spread before them, they took turns pinning the countries they each wanted to visit. Traveling partner Chris Monheim was adamant about India. She wanted to see if a boy she had been sponsoring through Christian Children's Fund had been receiving her help.

"I was sure that he didn't even exist," Caroline recalled, laughing. A few months later the two friends arrived in the village where they were greeted ceremoniously by women who showered them with rice and flowers. They found the child, Manus, doing well under CCF care. The local CCF contact, Damodar Sahoo, extended an invitation to his home for dinner. It was a meeting that would change both his and Caroline's lives.

"Nothing had prepared me for what I was about to

see," Caroline said that fall morning in Starbucks. Throngs of orphans ran to the car to greet their papa. The children swarmed the two Americans, climbing into their laps and wanting to play. And then Caroline met Sibani, who had been found abandoned in the bushes when she was five days old; and in that moment she found the thing that had been so desperately missing from her life – purpose.

"It hurt to think that she belonged to no one. I didn't know how, but I knew I had to act. The sound of her little bones hitting that wooden bed broke me. I couldn't believe she had to live that way." She looked at me over the now cold coffee and, four years later, her eyes filled with tears at the memory.

Leaving India with the children still haunting her, Caroline agonized, searched her soul and journaled about what she had seen. She knew her life had just taken a drastic turn off its previous course, although where it was headed and how exactly she was going to affect any change for Sibani and the other children was still unclear. Returning home early from the trip, rather than looking for a new job in advertising she embarked instead on a mission researching nonprofit agency guidelines and procedures. Discouraged by the myriad regulations and licensing requirements, for the first time Caroline thought maybe she really couldn't do it.

But waiting for her at home was a delivery package from Chris, with whom she had traveled. Pulling away the packing material, Sibani's eyes gazed up at her from the framed photo in her hand, on it Chris had written, "You can

do it!" Her purpose renewed, Caroline tackled the long and
brutal process of forming a nonprofit organization while
freelancing for income. Once the U.S. license was obtained,
she had to turn around and do it all over again in India.
Caroline took her last bit of savings and returned to the
orphanage, where she was amazed to find that the little
trickle of money she had been sending had already made a
major difference. "The kids were eating protein," she said.
This was a huge step forward from the rice and sugar that
had once constituted their entire diet.

Damodar Sahoo was shocked that Caroline had not
only sent money for the children, but that she had returned
just as fervently committed to the cause as ever. He insisted
from that time forward that she would call him Papa and
his wife, Mama. She was their daughter now, as surely as
any of the hundred children living there were.

Caroline realized what a huge impact could be made
for even larger numbers of kids if she could involve more
people in their lives. A goal for her new nonprofit began to
form – recruiting sponsors who would be committed to
these children throughout their childhoods. "I wanted to
give them resources and, even more importantly, a
surrogate family," she said. She put together a board of
directors for The Miracle Foundation and declared a
mission statement: "Empowering children to reach their full
potential, one orphan at a time."

The interview over, Caroline sat back and looked at me.
"Why don't you come to India with me?" she asked. Then
she waited.

It was all the encouragement I needed; immediately I knew I would go. I had entertained notions in the past of volunteering at a Russian or Romanian orphanage, or teaching English to children in rural Japan. At the time they had all seemed far-flung and impractical ideas. But, in that moment, I realized the problem had been that I had no real personal connection to any of those places or the people and organizations who worked in them. I replied with a completely inadequate reflection of my emotions at the prospect.

"Okay," I said, setting in motion five months of planning, travel arrangements, visas and inoculations. It was only after the trip when Caroline confided that at the time she asked me, she never thought I'd actually go. It wasn't a vacation or a sightseeing tour. It had been a difficult, exhausting and frequently heart-wrenching journey for her. And, even as she arranged a volunteer group, Caroline had trouble believing that anyone else would want to pay their way to go help with the work she had been doing for years.

Between October of 2004 and the following March, which our trip was scheduled for, an event of monumental impact occurred. Early on the morning after Christmas Day, in villages along the southern Indian coast, people stood on the shore and watched in fascination and horror as the water receded away from them, far out to sea. Soon it came rushing back with terrible destruction. The deadliest tsunami in history wiped out homes and entire villages and took with it more than ten thousand Indian lives.[viii]

Men from the fishing villages who had been at sea were washed away, and the land that used to give fruits and vegetables was rendered infertile for years. The people lost more than their property and loved ones. The ocean that was once their livelihood had become their greatest fear. Many of them would no longer go near the water.

In the weeks following the tsunami, housing became the biggest concern with hundreds of thousands left homeless. Childcare was also a difficulty because so many children had lost at least one parent. Numerous organizations flooded the area trying to get children adopted amid efforts to properly identify the dead and remaining family relations, and fears of child trafficking. The government began giving some of the international aid money to relatives to take in the children, or placing those without family into existing orphanages.

In the meantime, Caroline Boudreaux was hard at work in the United States raising more money to assist those affected by the disaster. She asked Dr. Manjeet S. Pardesi, a PhD Chartered Accountant in Delhi who had been hired to audit the orphanage and organization books, to help determine how The Miracle Foundation could best help. Dr. Pardesi traveled to Naggapattinam, the region most devastated by the tidal waves and flooding, to find out from the locals what their greatest needs were.

Dr. Pardesi proposed that the disaster relief funds raised by The Miracle Foundation – ultimately $40,000 – be used to build a village and daycare center, complete with park and playground. By the time we left for India in early

March, temporary homes had been built to house five hundred. The village was well received. It was the only post-tsunami operational facility within a thirty-mile radius. Daycare was run by social workers who held play therapy sessions with the children. Such a simple thing, but the play was a much-needed distraction for these smallest victims of the disaster. The children could swing and chase and laugh, escaping the loss of their parents, brothers, sisters and friends – if only for a few moments.

* * *

March 12, 2005

The plane from Delhi started its final descent for landing and my heart began to race. After thirty-six hours of travel this was the last leg of the journey. It brought me and ten other volunteers to Bhubaneswar, capital of the northeastern state of Orissa located four hundred kilometers south of Calcutta, where the Miracle Foundation orphanage director would meet us. As the plane touched down my stomach tightened. I waited impatiently for the exit doors to open. Eleven dazed Americans emerged into the piercing sunlight and walked across the tarmac to the small terminal. Caroline was immediately spotted by Damodar Sahoo – the man known to all simply as "Papa." In his white Punjabi suit that looked a bit like pajamas, he appeared just as the pictures I'd seen of him, only bigger. A large man, not fat but substantial, Papa swept Caroline into his arms for a hug across the metal bars separating the passengers in baggage claim from those waiting for them. He lifted his large, thick 1980s style glasses from the bridge of his nose and dabbed at his eyes with a handkerchief.

It was then that I saw he had an entourage. Behind him were his wife, two women staff members, and three girls from the home. They broke into huge smiles, waving excitedly and calling "Sister Caroline!" Caroline greeted and hugged them all while the rest of us gathered our luggage, our energy suddenly replenished. As we each showed our passport and exited the gate, the girls handed us bouquets of marigolds and red roses, then kissed their fingers and bent down to touch our feet in blessing. The oldest girl, Jhillismita – nicknamed Jilly – was about fourteen and wore a brilliant blue salwar kameez, the casual Indian outfit many girls of adolescence and older wear, comprised of a long top over matching pants and a scarf. The two younger girls, Pinky and Meena, were around seven years old and dressed in simple cotton floral schoolgirl dresses, with headbands holding back their short glossy hair. They were bashful with us, dropping their heads and giggling together when we tried to take photos with them.

Our group made its way outside as everyone else in the small airport stared after us. Two jeep-like vehicles were brought around for all eighteen of us and our piles of luggage. Long moments of delay followed while Papa and the drivers held a frenzied discussion. I stood by with the other volunteers pretending not to notice the passersby pointing us out to each other. I wasn't sure what the waiting and confusion were about, but after only a few hours and two airports I was beginning to understand they accompanied most everything in India. At last our luggage was crammed into one car and tied to the roof of another. Everyone piled in. We zoomed away from the airport, narrowly missing bicycles, pedestrians, cows and mopeds. Our driver, like all the others around him, merely laid on his horn continuously – presumably to warn those in his path that it would be their fault if they were struck, having been given adequate warning.

As we entered the city, the cacophony of sights and sounds that was Bhubaneswar was jarring after the peaceful countryside I had gazed down on from the airplane. From the air the beauty of the place was unmistakable - lush trees and hillsides, stands of palms along lakes and rivers. The green was a richer shade than I'd ever seen before, the water a serene silver mirror reflecting sky, the pure undeveloped land seemingly endless. Now, in the midst of it, there was no still or quiet space. Instead there were throngs of people everywhere, living and working and sleeping; hundreds of street vendors lined every available inch of sidewalk. The dusty roads peppered with potholes were filled with a constant stream of buses, bicycles, rickshaws, cars and cows. Rising over it all was the constant blaring beep-beep of the horns. It was the most alive place I had ever been.

Leaving Bhubaneswar we drove another twenty minutes before reaching the smaller city of Cuttack, near the orphanage. We stopped briefly at the hotel to check in and leave our bags before continuing on our way to Papa's ashram. Another careening ride down the bumpy roads and a drive across a curious toll bridge on which there was much exchange of words and then money, more waiting, until the gate was finally hand lifted by a guard. Night was falling as we lurched along and then, without warning, we turned in through the gates.

In a second, the cars stopped where rows of children were lined around the drive in a semi-circle, waving and chanting "welcome" over and over. I climbed out and they were all around me, touching my feet in blessing. Overwhelmed and unsure what to do, I blindly followed behind Papa and Caroline amidst the sea of small bodies. The children were shy at first, excited but reticent. One little girl of about seven summoned her courage. She touched my arm, then took my hand. "Hello," she said softly, looking up briefly before her eyes slid away from their contact with mine. As soon as she did this, the surrounding children shed their reserve and moved in close, putting their hands out for me to shake. I did, over and over; there was a never-ending supply of hands raised in front of me.

"Hello, hello," I greeted dozens of children who passed as a blur before me, the throng of us slowly making our way into the ashram. Everything seemed to be happening so quickly. I didn't have time to look around, to see the new wing The Miracle Foundation built or to get any sense of where I was in the darkness. There were just the children, all around, and my feet moving forward until we came to a courtyard. Then, as if as one, the kids left our sides and began climbing a staircase in an orderly fashion. We followed with the dozen or so staff, removing our shoes at the top of the stairs and entering the prayer room.

The children were already lined up and sitting on rugs, boys on one side and girls on the other, ages progressively going up toward the back with older kids sitting behind younger ones. Ceiling fans whirred overhead to stir up the warm air. We were escorted to the front of the room where we, too, sat cross-legged – male volunteers on the boys' side and female volunteers on the girls'. At the front of the room was an altar holding flowers, small trinkets of devotion, a picture of the guru Sai Baba and a statue of Vishnu, an ancient Hindu god. Tacked to the walls on all sides were pictures of other Hindu gods – Ganesh and Krishna – as well as Jesus, Mary, Mother Theresa and Mohammed. A staff member lit incense at the altar while another blew a horn softly. The children sat up straighter and ceased any fidgeting or whispering.

Papa walked to his brand-new podium and microphone, a contraption he was clearly proud of, and began to speak. Alternating between English and Oriya, the local dialect, he welcomed Caroline as his "daughter" and the volunteers as friends, introducing us one at a time. When Papa called my name, a girl I later learned was Sibani presented me with another bouquet and bent down to touch my feet.

Then the prayers began. It started with a simple chant: "Om....om..," the small voices resonating deeply. Finally things slowed down enough for me to begin to take it all in, to look at the kids clearly and in light, to start to feel my heart calm. The chanting gave way to a song, a hundred sweet voices dancing in the air and filling the room. Beside me on the rug sat one of the smallest girls, with glossy black curls and deep dimples. She was sitting lotus-style with her middle fingers and thumbs pressed together on the knees of her yellow and green flowered dress, eyes squinted tightly shut in concentration. Her strong, clear singing distinctly carried to my ears apart from the others. The voice of this three-year-old rising so pure and true was one of the most powerful sounds I had ever heard.

Soon the singing faded into silence and Papa prayed. He said there were many religions represented and respected in the ashram. "Here, there are Hindus, Christians, Buddhists and Muslims. We pray," Papa said, "to God and Allah and Jesus and Mohammed. The meaning of life is to love all. The purpose of life is to serve all."

It was a simple prayer, reminding me that life need not be complicated unless we made it so. A soothing peace palpable in the air filled me. I breathed out deeply. The past forty hours of travel and little sleep fell away as if they were nothing. There seemed no other world outside this place. Papa spoke as my eyes traveled over the faces all around me. I wondered when each of them had stopped wanting to go home, or if they ever had. As much of a loving community as the ashram seemed, it was not the family that most of the children had once known, now distant and ghostly memories for the most part.

Home is a fragile concept – far more delicate than those of us who have always had one can imagine. When a person no longer has a home, when his family is taken from him and he is deprived of everything that was familiar, then after a while wherever he is becomes home. Slowly, the pieces of memory fade, until this strange new place is not strange anymore; it becomes harder to recall the past life, a long ago family, until one day he realizes he *is* home.

---

viii Government of India, Ministry of Home Affairs, http://www.ndmindia.nic.in/Tsunami2004/sitrep35.htm.

"The ultimate tragedy is not the oppression and cruelty
by the bad people but the silence over that by the
good people."

–*Martin Luther King, Jr.*

You Bought Me Sleep

They are the lucky ones, these children. Far from the tourist's India of the Taj Mahal and yoga retreats, a journey into an Indian orphanage is a difficult one – hard on the body, hard on the heart. In homes like Papa's where children are well taken care of, it's far too easy to forget the street kids outside the gates, the children sleeping under plastic roofs beside a sewage-filled canal, the thirty thousand babies born HIV-positive each year.[ix] In the best of institutional homes there is love and community. Needs are met on the most basic sustenance levels. But, there seems to never be enough food, never adequate medical care. And never, ever enough room. For every child fortunate enough to live in a home like The Miracle Foundation provides, there are a thousand more the orphanage cannot afford to take in. A thousand who have nowhere to turn but homes run under vastly inferior, sometimes horrific conditions; a thousand more children living on the streets, begging at train stations, or working twelve hours a day for pennies - children for whom childhood has been discarded. Shunned by society and left to fend for themselves, they are the world's throwaways.

* * *

That first night I searched for a special child, Santosh. I had recruited a friend to sponsor him and we had received photos and letters from the nine-year-old boy. After prayers the children and volunteers were led back downstairs to the courtyard for snacks and chai, the rich black spiced tea with lots of milk and sugar. A few sprinkles of rain fell as we sat under a large mango tree, and the summer night air turned cool. I asked about Santosh.

"Santosh! Where is Santosh?" Papa asked, and sent a worker off to find him. Soon the boy appeared, reluctantly trudging forward. He was slightly built, wearing a green and beige checked button-down shirt and blue shorts, his knees dusty beneath the hem of the shorts. His hair had grown out considerably from the nearly buzz cut of the photograph I had. It was now parted on the side and combed neatly across his forehead. He barely looked at me as Papa explained that I was here representing his sponsor. I shook Santosh's hand, told him how happy I was to meet him and asked for a picture together. He stood beside my chair stoically, his body stiff under the arm I placed across his shoulders, unsmiling as the camera clicked. He appeared bashful or embarrassed to be singled out, running off as soon as the photo was taken.

Santosh had been brought to the home just before his second birthday, a boy who could not have any real memories of his previous family, but must have missed them just the same. His mother had died. His father remarried. The official admittance report stated that after his father wed, he "was staying in another place leaving Santosh helpless and alone, because the second mother of Santosh did not agree to keep the child with her." An ex-resident of the orphanage, another who had been taken in as a child and grown up to a more promising future, learned of Santosh's plight and brought him to Papa.

I thought Santosh was too shy to interact with me and I wouldn't see much of him during the week we would be there. But I was wrong. He was simply not used to the attention and had difficulty grasping the idea that someone had come from across the world just to visit him. It was a powerful thing to walk into a place like this and call out a child's name. It says I am here for *you*, to these children for whom no one has ever come looking. To be sought out, to realize that someone else knows they exist, says *you matter*.

Moments later Santosh was back, smiling uncertainly up at me. I hugged him, patting his shoulder. He remained by my side, never leaving it again except once more – he darted off and returned wearing a baseball cap that was sent from his sponsor, my friend Craig. He pressed against my chair, claiming his spot, as other children crowded around.

There was Sibani again, the little girl who had inspired everything we were doing. In my mind I pictured the filthy toddler Caroline first met nearly five years ago, sitting next to her one plate of rice and water for the day, unsmiling and exhausted. But in front of me was a precocious seven-year-old who giggled constantly, revealing even white baby teeth. Her short boy haircut allowed her twinkling eyes to be the most striking feature about her face. Standing before me in a yellow jumper dress, she held her fist up with index and pinky fingers pointing out. Sibani took my hand and made the same sign, pressing my fingertips against hers. Then, our thumbs came down to meet and she twisted our wrists until our hands clasped. I was delighted – it was a secret handshake! At once all the kids standing around wanted to do it, pushing each other out of the way for their chance with me.

When the time came to leave for the night, a goodbye parade occurred much like the welcome one. Again I shook dozens of little hands. "Good night!" they proudly said in English.

"See you tomorrow," I told them, and some of the braver kids replied, "Tomorrow!"

Santosh was still by my side as I climbed into the jeep, holding his hand through the open window. He grinned at me and touched the bill of his cap. We all gave a final wave and were out the gates, as I wondered how I would ever sleep that night.

* * *

The next morning, the volunteers gathered for Papa to lead us on a tour of his ashram. There were Baxter and Matt, both self-employed single men; Anna and Andy, newlyweds who had decided to make this trip a special kind of honeymoon; friends Lara and Rae; and Kathleen, an advertising executive who knew Caroline from her previous life in advertising. All, like me, were from Austin. Also on the trip was Diane from Dallas, a close friend of Caroline's, and her teenage son, Chris; the only ones in our group who had made the journey before. We were all sponsors of children or donors and supporters of The Miracle Foundation.

As Papa guided us around the compound we were able to see, in the light of day, what had been a mystery the night before. We started at the newest addition, the teacher compound where young women lived for several months at a time training to be schoolteachers. Their quarters surrounded a charming courtyard with colorful saris hanging from the upstairs balcony. The teaching students peeked from windows and doorways as we filed through. Papa showed us the classrooms, explaining the daily schedule written on a large board outside. His black hair gleamed in the sun and his salt-and-pepper mustache danced above his lips as he bombarded us with information.

"The children wake up at five a.m. and wash. At six a.m. is morning prayer; then they eat breakfast and go to class," Papa said as he moved down the daily agenda. "After school lessons, in the afternoon there are chores, games, evening prayers, study time and then dinner. Bedtime is nine-thirty."

Turning from the blackboard, he insisted, "Come, come!" as he led us to the dormitories. Boys and girls were awaiting us on their bunk beds in each room, chanting "Welcome" as soon as we entered. On the cement floors were chalk drawings, flowers and big hearts in which they had written "We love Caroline Didi" and "Welcome Caroline Didi and Volunteers."

"Didi means sister in Hindi," Caroline explained.

Our shoes were removed, put back on, and shed again as we moved from building to building. The brand new bathrooms were a wonder for this village, where running water wasn't even the norm. Only slightly more than one-third of the population has piped household water and less than eighteen percent of rural households in the state of Orissa have electricity.ˣ Papa gave thanks to God and The Miracle Foundation for these improvements, seemingly in equal measure.

Kids followed us, rushing past each other to claim a volunteer's hand. In the ashram the children were a constant presence. They were everywhere, always underfoot, craving our attention. As I walked along four or five were on each arm; every time I sat down there were children filling my lap, their slight frames making barely an imprint against my skin, or simply touching me as they stood close – small hands constantly on my arms, shoulders, feet.

These kids, who had so little compared to me, were still joyful and filled with hope. They shared and worked together, laughed and played and argued like a huge group of siblings. They possessed the least in terms of material possessions, yet were willing to share all they had. They offered seconds and thirds of their precious food, serving us before eating themselves. They rushed to bring water, pull up a chair for us, take our shoes off and put them back on, carry our bags – anything and everything.

It was clear that Papa and Caroline were doing something special here, something more than what could be seen with the eyes. Papa was the heart of the ashram and had created an almost tangible presence of love. Since the day I met her Caroline told me that Papa was the kindest man she had ever known. Gandhi and Jesus rolled into one and walking the earth was how she described him. She often said, "There is God, then there is Papa, and then there is everyone else."

Papa's life of service to children began in 1972 when he was working in distress relief, responsible for helping people maneuver through such disasters as droughts, floods, and earthquakes. One day while going about his work after a cyclone had hit, he found an orphaned child lying on the roadside next to her dead mother. Shortly thereafter a severe flood left another sixteen local children homeless and parentless. Mr. Sahoo and his wife welcomed them all into their own tiny home, caring for them in addition to their own daughter and two sons. Over the next twenty-five years, the children continued to arrive, until dozens came to know the Sahoo family as home.

Damodar "Papa" Sahoo was, at first appearance, deceptively simple. Unprepossessing, he greeted everyone heartily, chewing the betel nut that turned his teeth red. "I am so happy to have you here – you are all my children now," he proclaimed, then hacked and spit. *This is the sage?* I couldn't help thinking.

But, when Papa spoke of the children, his heart spilled from his mouth and with his words his wisdom, his infinite love and compassion for them was undeniable. The tour over, he urged us into his little office, seating us like pupils in front of him. Milli, a housemother, brought a tray of sodas as Papa began a speech. He had given up a far easier life and job as a government official to dedicate himself to these orphans. Paid a very small allowance as the director of the home, it was not an easy existence. He didn't seem to regard himself as remarkable or noble, however, and appeared detached from all things material.

"I am a simple beggar," he said, his eyes boring into me to confirm that I didn't doubt his words. "I need nothing, except for these children, my family."

Over the past few years as Caroline raised money for the orphanage, building a new wing and bunk beds and bathrooms for the children, she repeatedly asked Papa to let The Miracle Foundation make some improvements to his small quarters. To give him something that would make his life a little easier.

"Let me do something for you," she told Papa.

"No, no, I need nothing," he answered always.

"Let me buy you something," Caroline persisted.

But Papa only shook his head, gesturing toward the new dormitories and the children in their uniforms going to school. "You have already bought me the most important thing," he said. "You bought me sleep."

* * *

The bell rang for lunch and everyone appeared again in the courtyard just outside Papa's office, holding their aluminum plates. Although meals were usually eaten in the dining hall, today rugs were unrolled on the cement floor of the courtyard so that children and volunteers could eat together. We sat along the rugs as the staff worked their way down the rows with huge pots of food, spooning rice onto each plate, then vegetables and finally dal, the lentil bean sauce which is a staple of the Indian subcontinent. The kids waited patiently for all to be served and the prayer to be sung. Then we ate.

Silence descended as the children quickly scooped up food with their fingers. When I was provided a spoon the group of middle school age boys I sat among laughed at the Westerner and her crazy ways. The kids ate intently, accepting seconds and thirds as leftovers were taken around. I had never seen such tiny people eat so much. As they finished, they hopped up one by one and ran off to wash their plates.

Papa came around with sweets for the volunteers. Walking to Caroline first, he picked something out of the bowl with his fingers and popped it right into her mouth. He did the same to each of us in turn.

"You taste!" he instructed as he launched a round, brown pastry into my mouth. It was sweet, all right – sort of like a donut hole soaked in molasses. It was my first taste of Gulab Jamun, and it squeaked loudly between my teeth as I chewed. I swallowed it down, smiling and thanking Papa.

All of the children had left their places except one. Little Salu, the three-year-old of the dimples and curls whose singing voice had carried so sweetly during prayers the night before. Only she remained, sitting with her plate in the middle of the near-empty courtyard, her cheeks puffed and rounded with food.

* * *

That afternoon Anna, the volunteer on her "honeymoon," and I set up artwork stations with sketch pads, coloring pencils and jumbo boxes of crayons. The kids stared at the boxes in amazement, selecting only one crayon each with reticence as if this windfall might be taken away at any moment. We began to make friends, discovering they were just as curious about us and our lives as we were about them. Children spoke varying levels of English, largely dependent on how many years they had been living in the ashram and attending school. Some had a large vocabulary and conversational skills; others spoke little more than a few words of English. I found it was surprisingly easy, however, to communicate with children without sharing even a word of common language.

They hovered over the books, coloring with all the intensity of da Vinci painting the Mona Lisa. With encouragement, they each soon had a stack of crayons beside them. They began to hoard them, fighting over the colored sticks. I moved around the room, monitoring and refereeing the crayon situation while admiring finished masterpieces held in front of me by dozens of little hands.

"Didi! Didi!" called one voice after another, often several at once as they clamored for me to notice them. They came in groups, younger boys then older; then the girls. Some of the coloring books had pages of stickers, which I peeled off and stuck on the boys' shirts. They wore them proudly, like badges. Soon the stickers were all over the arms and faces of boys of all ages. You wouldn't catch many teenage American boys allowing this, or at least not showing that they liked it, but these kids were having a blast. Santosh stayed near me, remaining even after the boys left and girls began filing in.

Two young girls in particular crowded beside me wherever I was, squeezing into the most impossibly small spaces between me and another child in order to sit next to me. They eagerly showed me drawing after drawing, five and six and then seven, beaming in satisfaction when I oohed and aahed over them. I learned that they were sisters. The older of the two was Sumi, who had a large bandage patched across her lower right cheek and jaw. When I inquired later Papa told me she had an infection. The younger girl was Mami. They both shared the same chubby cheeks and liquid brown eyes that seemed impossibly big for their faces. They wore matching black and red floral dresses with ruffled collars and untied sashes that hung limply along their legs.

I turned the girls around to tie the sashes and saw that the backs of their dresses gaped open – all the buttons were missing and the dresses were held together with a safety pin at the nape of the neck. It seemed such a small thing, but clearly demonstrated the minimal basics of necessity that defined the ashram as well as the lack of personal attention these kids received, impossible in a home with more than one hundred children and a dozen adults.

"Didi, look!" said Sumi, tugging on my sleeve as she proudly displayed the pink flowers she had drawn.

When the art was put away, a group of adolescent girls led by Srabani took me by the hand and dragged me past their dormitory to a small temple in the middle of the ashram. Srabani, a beautiful and intelligent girl of fifteen who spoke excellent English, explained that this was the "cyclone temple." In 1999 a cyclone had swept through Orissa, destroying virtually the entire compound. Everything was reduced to rubble – all except the statue of the god Shiva, which was left sitting inside this temple completely untouched.

Shiva is the Destroyer, aptly enough named. In India there are many gods and goddesses that have been born of the Hindu religion and folklore, all considered faces of the all-knowing divine God. Similar to the Christian belief in Jesus Christ as the human incarnation of God, in Hinduism there are multiple avatars of the Supreme Being. There is

Ganesh, the elephant god of intellect and the arts. Vishnu is the preserver, the essence of all beings. The goddess Lakshmi represents wealth and fortune; I had noticed many shops named with variations of Lakshmi.

I likened them to the saints of the Christian world; devotees prayed to different saints for different reasons – health or prosperity and so on. Through prayer time and Papa's inclusion of all religions and deities, I had a great appreciation for the Hindu belief that all spiritual paths were equally valid. There seemed a god and goddess for everything – and everyone. Shiva sat serenely inside the small blue temple, flower petals strewn around him, and gazed out at us dispassionately. Like all the other gods, he was eternal.

* * *

With the other volunteers I spent the next few days just being with the kids, befriending them, playing with them. Our days at the ashram were filled with games, reading, dancing and laughing. It felt a lot like summer camp. There were puzzles, English flash cards, hopscotch, frisbee and the hokey-pokey, which the kids wanted to do over and over once it was taught to them. When it was time to "put your backside in and shake it all about" they shook for all it was worth and giggled like mad.

Baxter and Matt, two of the male volunteers, had bought a length of rope at a local shop and set up a tug-of-war. We stretched it out in the play yard and divided boys into two teams. After a quick demonstration and instructions they played the first round, cheering when a side won and quickly setting up again for round two. Heels dug in, they waited for the word "go!" and started pulling with all their might. About a minute into it, without warning the burlap rope snapped in two, right down the middle. At the sudden slack, both teams fell to the ground where they sat a second, stunned, before rolling in the dirt with laughter.

I began to discover who the kids were – their individual personalities and dreams. I watched the shy ones come out of their shells and self-confidence blossom. As it did, their "best behavior" fell away and they were normal kids, not always sweet and perfect but often mischievous as well. When they thought I wasn't looking, they would shove each other out of the way or bestow thunks on one another's heads in annoyance. They used the language barrier to their advantage, pretending at times not to understand when the adult volunteers said it was time to put a game away, reminding me of my daughter when she was young and seemingly deaf to the word "no."

Rashikanta, a high-energy boy of about twelve with extremely thick hair and close-set eyes, delighted in playing pranks on me. He liked to move my bag and watch me search for it. When we played with clay one afternoon, he ran up with a wad of the gray stuff in his hands, handing it to me so I could fashion something with it. But when I squeezed the clay, water squirted out of it and all over my lap. Rashikanta bent over double with glee; he had hollowed out the ball of clay and filled it with water just to play the trick on me.

Mami and Sumi grabbed my hands and led me, along with the other women volunteers, into their dorm. Girls poured into the rooms as they pulled out powder and lipstick, henna and face paints and went to work on us. Two hovered with the henna over Rae's and Lara's arms and two more over their feet. Sukru, a quiet older teenager who held her hands in front of her mouth when she smiled, sat in front of me and patted powder all over my face while Srabani did the same to Kathleen. On top of the powder Sukru placed a jeweled bindi, the decorative Hindu dot, between my eyes and began to paint intricate designs above my eyebrows.

She and the other girls who crowded around asked me curious questions – how many brothers and sisters did I have, how old was I, was I married? They asked what my parent's names were, their mouths twisting with effort as they repeated my answer. "Chaw-lie Sall, Sun-dee Sall," they said, then broke into laughter at the funny-sounding names, so hard to pronounce. Someone turned on a radio and a few girls sprang up to dance, performing MTV-like moves in unison to the Hindi pop music. It was just like slumber parties I had attended when I was their ages, a couple dozen girls laughing, dancing and playing with makeup. When the four volunteers were powdered, painted and hennaed the girls paraded us into the courtyard proudly to show off their handiwork. It was the most fun I'd had in a long time.

Then the dinner bell rang and we gathered in the
courtyard for the adult meal. As we ate Mrs. Sahoo, or
Mama as she insisted we call her, brought out small bowls
of a custard. Not having spoons or forks at this meal, we
couldn't figure out how to eat it with our hands. Of course
Papa had to show us; unfortunately he chose me to
demonstrate, marching over to my seat. I braced myself
because I already had a mouth full of chicken and rice. Papa
took my flat bread and dipped it into the custard.

"You see?" he asked as he shoved the end of it into my
mouth. I had so much food in my mouth I could barely
chew and although the custard was delicious, it wasn't so
tasty mixed with the dal. I caught sight of Caroline across
the circle of chairs, trying to control her laughter.

* * *

We were the only Westerners in the town; I hadn't seen
a single other since arriving in Cuttack. Everyone stared
constantly and we created a spectacle wherever we went.
Walking from the hotel a quarter-mile to the internet café,
groups of schoolgirls followed me. Other shoppers spied on
me surreptitiously, curious about the water or bangles I
might buy. I stopped at a vendor stall one afternoon to ask
if they had foil packets of henna I could purchase for the
girls. The floor space of the small shop was covered in bags
of grain and bushels of beans, and the shelves were filled
with everything from shampoo to candy bars. As one
shopkeeper added up my purchase another posed the
common question: "Where from?"

"The United States," I answered. "Texas."

"Oh, George Bush," he replied knowingly. Then he asked, "Is close to Chicago?"

One morning Milli and Madhu, two of the housemothers, offered to take the volunteers shopping. Our list included hair barrettes and bindis for all the girls and a new sari for Mama. A frail, bird-like woman who felt as if she'd break in two with a hug, Mama was frequently ill and spent most of her time in private quarters.

We also wanted our own comfortable salwar kameez to wear around the ashram. The week had progressively gotten hotter as summer arrived in earnest, and the Indian style of dressing seemed much cooler and more practical.

Four of us joined Madhu and Milli in our hotel lobby. Madhu was petite and impish, with a round face and mischievous twinkle in her eyes. Milli was one of the most elegant women I had ever met. Soft spoken and beautiful, her dark hair waved softly back from her pale face. She carried herself with the grace and poise of royalty, gorgeous saris floating around her, which had earned her our nickname "Floating Milli."

We set off with the driver, winding through chaotic streets until we were quite sure we were lost; then suddenly, at Milli's command, the driver stopped in front of a store. Kathleen, Lara, Rae and I tried on salwar suits while Madhu and Milli watched over us like mother hens. Next was the sari shop. Floor-to-ceiling shelves were stacked with folded sarees of every color and pattern imaginable, and the three shopkeepers pulled down one after another, unfolding their splendor on the counters. Some Milli simply waved away dismissively, saying "No, no." Others she turned to ask our opinion. "You like?" After much consideration we made our selection and were on our way again, across the street to the last stop of the day.

Here we spent half an hour choosing hair clips and bindis as the shopkeepers brought out box after box of bangles and earrings for us to consider, trying to make a bigger sale from the Americans. Finally we were ready, but the shopkeepers wouldn't tally our sales. We pulled out rupees, but the young woman of the shop seemed unable to take the money, recruiting one of the men. He finally began the tally – by hand, writing each separate bindi and barrette individually on a piece of paper in spite of the fact that they were all the same price.

We had hundreds of them. Fifteen minutes dragged by, then thirty, but there was nothing to be done. The heat in the shop became thick; it was past two in the afternoon and none of us had eaten lunch. The counting continued. The shopkeepers brought out stools for us to sit on.

The Indian concept of time had been explained to me in one of the countless parables that weave through the culture's long history. Legend has it there is a great raven with a scarf clasped in its beak, which flies over the Himalayas once every thousand years. As it soars past, the scarf scrapes a bit of snow off the top of the mountains. Eventually, the Himalayas will be worn down and completely scraped away. This, however, will take a very long time. Indian time is relative. What exists in the earth will long outlast us and endure. There is never any hurry for anything, never any rush.

After almost an hour the counting was finally done and the total announced. Four thousand, two hundred rupees. Up until that moment I had been amazed by how inexpensive everything was in comparison to U.S. standards. A twenty-minute phone call home from the corner store was fifty rupees - little more than a dollar. Half an hour at the internet cafe, ten rupees - about a quarter. Tandoori chicken, rice and tea at the hotel, a hundred-thirty rupees, or four dollars. Four thousand two hundred rupees, however, equated to over a hundred dollars. No, no, this couldn't be. It was far too much and Milli vehemently protested. We put back half the bindis as Milli continued to argue. The counting began anew. Madhu sent a boy down the street to bring back juice. The four wimpy Americans were fading fast.

After what seemed an eternity an agreement was reached, money changed hands, and we were finally off with our gifts for fifty little girls. The six of us temporarily parted ways at the hotel as new friends.

* * *

In the midst of the games, laughter and silliness that we engaged in all day long it was sometimes easy for me to forget that these children were orphans. When that reality came crashing back it never failed to hurt my insides with the same breathless intensity as it had the first time.

Especially when it intruded unexpectedly, as happened later that afternoon.

Caroline and Papa had arranged an ice cream party. Two tables were pulled into the courtyard as the frozen cartons were delivered. The kids lined up eagerly from youngest to oldest to be handed their paper cups of ice cream as we scooped it out in a battle of time against the sun blazing overhead. As we served the icy treats and listened to the kids slurping away, I noticed that Santosh was nowhere to be seen. I asked some of the other boys about him, and they pointed toward the top of the stairs.

I went up and found him sitting alone, seeming sad and listless. He wasn't interested in the ice cream. Madhu passed and I asked her to help me find out what was wrong; I was afraid Santosh was hurt, or sick. Madhu took him into the boys' dorm and talked to him for several minutes.

"He misses his mother," she said simply when she came back out.

I felt it in my heart, and knew that although they loved us being there, it could sometimes only make them miss the presence of their own parents. The good of all these caring surrogate parent figures – Papa, Caroline, the housemothers, the volunteers – outweighed the heaviness of sorrow, to be sure. But, at times, one could easily miss the sadness, in the presence of the love that filled the ashram. I was reminded anew that these children all carried secret grief and damage inside them, often hidden or temporarily forgotten but never erased entirely.

I sat with Santosh on the edge of the concrete walkway outside his dorm room. Draping my arm around his shoulders, I squeezed reassuringly and held him against my side. I knew that his mother had died when he was so young he couldn't possibly remember her, not really. Nonetheless, to mourn the idea of a mother, that huge absence in his life, like a great gaping hole – that was another thing entirely. We sat together, not speaking, while in the courtyard in front of us the other children slurped up their ice cream noisily.

---

ix UNICEF website, "Real Lives: Keeping Infants Safe in India," http://www.unicef.org/infobycountry/india_2044.html.
x Outlook India, "State of the Nation: Damned Statistics," April 9, 2007.

"A small body of determined spirits fired by an
unquenchable faith in their mission can alter the course
of history."

–Mahatma Gandhi

India's Spell

India was everything I had imagined it would be – only more so. More colors and smells, more noises and people, more everything. It was an assault on all the senses at once. Its sweeping history as the last of the great early civilizations, in existence alongside ancient Greece and Babylon, had survived virtually unchanged in many places and in many ways. While in other ways, it became one of the most rapidly evolving nations in the world. India was too big to describe adequately, perhaps too big to absorb in a single lifetime. The country wrapped itself around me, refusing to let go.

Chanting from nearby temples wafted up to my hotel room along with the sandalwood smell of incense. The woman of the house outside my window was on her rooftop terrace every morning hanging laundry and watering plants. When I opened the window the sounds of India rushed in. They were now-familiar sounds I knew I would miss. Dogs barking, children laughing, prayers being sung, the beep-beep of horns, and underneath it all – one had to listen carefully for it – the swoosh-swoosh of the brooms constantly brushing away the dust of Cuttack.

There was also what everyone, including myself, expected of India – despair, filth, destitution. All were things that caused some people to question why I would ever want to come; the things that so many visitors to India recoiled from. The trash that lined the roads and the beggars that tapped at car windows. The deteriorating buildings, the ragged street vendors, the ramshackle homes for which *hut* was too grandiose a term. The frantic poverty that does not let you rest.

Still, there was beauty in the midst of it – the parts of India those well-meaning people had not considered or could not see. The vitality of life teeming all around, the jangling of bangles and ankle bracelets, the colorful saris, the carved temples, with swaying trees surrounding it all. The tremendous scale of its monuments and palaces and art left one stunned, as did the strange way there was a deep-seated peace even in the midst of tumultuous movement and clamor. The wonderful and the abject coexisted side by side. Though the country struggled with the indigence of large numbers of its population, it was far from a poor place.

India had taught me something new – that beauty was not its own thing which could be separated out, sanitized, and kept apart for its own sake. Real beauty became diluted in that very process. It could not be fully seen and appreciated in that realm, so far removed from anything to compare it with, to cause it to fully stand out and be vibrant. The true measure of beauty lay in its imperfections; to see it, one must embrace it all. My previous American version of beauty seemed remote, generic, anesthetized; requiring an ever-higher standard before it could be realized. The simple truth of it was overlooked – but not here. Here, beauty could be found in a single raindrop, one golden sari, a flower in a tiny hand. I saw beauty in the way a well-tended dog was lovingly held in the lap of his Indian mistress. I saw beauty in the brief glimpse of the ornate interior of a Hindu temple, candles glowing and people bowing their heads to the ground in prayer.

Above all, this was India. And in the children this beauty seemed to come alive, almost making me believe it was a living entity I could capture in my hands.

The dinner bell rang, and the kids darted off to wash their hands and retrieve their metal plates. On this night we had been given the special honor of serving dinner. Children filed into the dining hall and took their places on the floor mats, waiting patiently as we carried pots of rice, dal and vegetables down the rows. I had never seen such discipline and manners among a group of kids this large. Matt and I were serving from a huge container of rice. As I scooped it out the rice stuck to the spoon with only a little falling off onto the plate. I dug out more spoonfuls while the children motioned their hands over their plates to indicate they didn't need more. I had watched these kids eat, shoveling the food quickly between fingers to mouths and taking seconds or thirds, so I knew it wasn't that they were not hungry. They were simply unselfish, wanting to make sure there was plenty for everyone else first.

Driving back late from the ashram, there seemed to be even more traffic of bicycles, rickshaws, cars and mopeds than during the day. The shops and stalls were still open, and music wafted in from everywhere. We crossed what we affectionately called the "Fred Flintstone Bridge" – the toll booth where sometimes we paid and sometimes we didn't, where the gate arm was weighted on one end by bricks and raised on the other by a guard loosening the rope. Driving alongside the river, ahead of us we saw a large group of people walking down the middle of the road, carrying candles and singing. Some were holding a white-shrouded object over their heads.

"You guys, it's a funeral procession," Caroline said. We pulled to the side to let them pass, maybe thirty or forty people holding the body aloft, draped in cloth and flowers. "They'll make a pyre to burn the body, then dump it in the river," she explained. I watched the procession pass in silence as I thought about the children I had seen earlier in the day bathing in that river, the cooking utensils washed there, the pails being drawn from it. The chanting grew faint behind us as the last white robes disappeared into the night.

* * *

The next morning in the car Caroline circulated lists of all the children. One by one, we made sure everyone was

accounted for and that all the letters and photographs sent
by sponsors were being distributed correctly. The shortest
list, a separate page with about a dozen names, looked
different from the others.

"What's this?" I asked.

Caroline glanced at it over my shoulder. "Those are
kids who don't have sponsors. Some of them are new;
others just haven't been sponsored yet."

I hadn't realized there were still unsponsored children,
and scrutinized the list more carefully to see if I recognized
any of the names. One jumped out at me – Daina, a five-
year-old who had become one of the pack of little girls,
along with Sibani and sisters Mami and Sumi, who
followed me constantly. Every time I turned around, or sat
down, they were there.

One evening as the sun was dimming in the sky, I was
sitting in the courtyard catching my breath after an endless
round of the hokey-pokey. The little girl group gathered
around. Mami and Sumi stood at each shoulder, playing
with my hair and jingling my earrings. Sibani and Daina
planted themselves in front of me and began to sing. They
started with "Twinkle, Twinkle, Little Star" and then moved
on to "Row, Row, Row Your Boat" and another tune I
didn't recognize. Their soft little sing-song voices had
drifted up into the night air as they continued their
repertoire.

I handed the list back to Caroline. "I'll sponsor
whichever of these kids picks *me*," I said. "Whoever seems
the most attached to me, that's who I want to sponsor."

Rohit, our driver, pulled the car to the side of the
narrow, crowded road and parked. This morning before
going to the ashram, our group had been invited to
breakfast at Major General Basant Kumar Mohapatra's
house. After forty years in the Indian Army the retired
Major General had dedicated his life to social services. A
long-time advocate for Papa's orphanage, he also supported
an old age home for the destitute.

We entered the gates of his courtyard from the dusty,
noisy street and instantly peace and beauty prevailed. The
landscaped garden was lush, the portico and covered patio
with rocking chairs inviting. The general shook our hands
and introduced us to his wife.

"Please, call me Aja," he said. Meaning "grandfather"
in Hindi, "Aja" was an address of both respect and
endearment. He led us inside with the same entreaty Papa
always used: "Come, come!" We sat in the cool living room,
fans blowing above and doors open to the fragrant garden
breezes.

Aja spoke of the children. His top priority was
education – they would have no hope for their futures
unless they learned English well and had a trade.
Improving their school, increasing English tutoring, and
providing vocational training or university as they reached
adulthood was paramount.

"They will be able to make a living if they have the
education to be carpenters, electricians, mechanical
repairmen or computer programmers," he said. I thought of
the article I had just read in the morning's paper about

Bangalore, the high-tech center of India, not having enough people to fill all their IT positions.

Aja was also concerned about giving the children what he called "appropriate technology." Most people in India live without amenities such as air conditioning, and it was doubtful the children would experience them again. "Why raise their level of expectation, get them acclimated to these luxuries as a standard, when in all likelihood they will not have them later?" Aja asked. "The goal is for each child to be fully prepared for a normal life in India; and so the focus is on basic needs, love and education – not amenities."

After being here only a short time, I understood the concern. It was this American acceptance of luxuries as standard conveniences, and then necessities, that led many of us into a pursuit of happiness in which the wanting of ever more ultimately leaves us unfulfilled. The condition has become so entrenched in our society that a term was coined for it: affluenza. Defined as an addiction to materialism or overconsumption, affluenza was the subject of a 1997 PBS documentary[xi] and its producer, John De Graaf, later co-wrote a bestselling book, *Affluenza: The All-Consuming Epidemic.*[xii] We often have everything we need and beyond, yet seem unable to satisfy our desire for more. The culture of consumerism is also one of great waste. The U.S. consumes eighty percent of the world's resources, while eighty percent of the rest of the world lives much the way I was seeing all around me here. Waste is even seen a status symbol. People waste simply to show that they can afford it, to show off to other people that they have the money and resources to do so. It was an embarrassment of riches.

There were many things Aja respected and admired about my home country – our pursuit and reward of personal excellence, the opportunity for a person of any class to improve their station in life. Many other things he found difficult to understand, such as our preoccupation with money and our complicated lifestyle.

"True wealth," he concluded, "lies not in wanting more, but in needing less." Being here, I had begun see my own culture, my own beliefs, in a whole new light and re-evaluate them. There was much to be learned in this place.

We were called into breakfast where we were served a delicious assortment of tiny filled pancake-like treats, vegetable-and-spice stuffed rolls, flat bread with mango chutney, and other exotic dishes. We talked leisurely over the meal for more than an hour and I found myself enjoying the relaxing pace, not missing the hectic, constantly harried rush that was my life back home. Our group discussed many things, but the conversation always came back to the children.

"They're so happy," Matt said, echoing the unexpected gift I also felt I'd received by being admitted into the circle of their simple joy. "It humbles me how much they want to share with me. Love is enough here."

Aja nodded. "It is because they know you come without any self-interest. You come only with love. This is the most important thing. Skin doesn't matter, color doesn't matter; only the heart matters. You come to share joy with them – and also sadness, if it is there." Santosh flashed into my mind, sitting on the step forlornly, missing a mother he had never really known. Yes, I had shared both their joys and sorrows.

Aja looked around the table at all of us. "Our support system is a family system, and you are part of the family now." Then he beamed, "You see, the world has become a global village."

* * *

The time to return home came much too quickly, just as I was beginning to feel a symmetry of place. The chaos was almost starting to seem normal to me, the maze of streets making sense as we left the hotel each morning. I recognized stalls and vendors and knew where we would turn. What had seemed such mayhem when we first arrived, I could now see had a certain rhythm and organization and I was growing strangely at home in the midst of it. And of course, there were the children. I was already sad at the thought of leaving.

For our last day with the kids a special outing had been arranged. With two rented buses we would drive to the other side of Bhubaneswar, about an hour away, to visit a wildlife park and botanical gardens. When the vehicles carrying the volunteers pulled through the ashram gates, the buses were already loaded and the kids were eager with anticipation. A few extra piled in the SUV – Santosh and two other adolescent boys, Asap and Bikram, sat with me in the back of the vehicle and bounced around on the seats in excitement.

The zoo was scenic and filled with exotic animals. Asian elephants, antelope, tigers and crocodiles roamed behind their fences, as the ever-present wild monkeys scampered loose between our feet and frolicked in the branches above us. Even though these were all native animals, it was the first time most of the children had ever seen the real thing. Many of the creatures had been injured or otherwise endangered when they were brought to the park, including a leopard captured when it was discovered loose in a public toilet in Cuttack.

The day quickly became the hottest yet. We sought out spots of shade along the way, trying to shelter ourselves from the blistering white-hot sun. Under a tree with huge spreading branches Papa unpacked cookies and bananas, still on the stalk, he had brought for snacks. I began to notice the looks we were getting from others at the wildlife park, happy Indian families on holiday or an outing with their children. At first we volunteers barely registered the stares; we were used to the locals' open curiosity. But these were looks of disdain, distaste and they were not only directed toward us, but the children as well. The orphans in their worn clothing, dozens of dresses and shirts made from the same material, some barefoot – and the Americans who were holding these untouchable hands, who were bringing them to this place that was for real families. Some people moved across the path or far out of the way to avoid coming too close to the children, as if their predicament were contagious.

Most of our kids had come from the lower castes. Even if they hadn't, being an orphan relegates one to untouchability, a status Gandhi had attempted to eradicate but whose stigma continues. Pinky, one of the younger girls who met us at the airport, was from the highest Brahmin caste – a distinction which had disappeared along with her family. The caste system in India is deep, pervasive and complicated. Its origins in the Hindu religion go back two thousand years to when the Brahmin priests declared that everyone had a preordained station in life, placing themselves at the top of the system and creating a rigid hierarchy by which lower citizens would be fit only for undesirable positions in society. They did the jobs not fit for the "forward" (upper) castes – duties such as the butchering of meat and toilet cleaning.

The Brahmins, wealthy landowners, and others belonging to the forward caste enjoyed what amounted to centuries of slave labor. Lower, or scheduled, caste members were not allowed to pass by the homes of the forward caste or even walk in their shadows. They were often required to sweep away their own footprints so the higher caste would not have to walk in their footsteps. In this fashion they became invisible, as if they didn't exist at all. This system permeated for ages and became greatly internalized by Indians at all caste levels.

Soon after the country's independence in 1947, the practice of untouchability was outlawed. Government regulations regarding caste were put into place to act as a sort of affirmative action, providing a certain number of places in universities and the government for members of the lower caste tribes. It was supposed to last only five to ten years, providing a method - under Gandhi's vision of a caste-free India - of protecting the scheduled caste members, giving them a foothold on the rung of the ladder of equality.

In the sixty years since, however, it hasn't quite worked out that way. Discrimination against Dalits, at one time considered the "untouchables," is pervasive. It is a complex mix of ethnic and class distinction, with the same dangers and abuses that racism and classism carry everywhere. The caste system is not fundamentally different than the legacy of institutionalized racism in the United States – a social problem that is still prevalent today, and only fifty years ago was legally protected and brutal discrimination rampant.

Just as in India one can often tell a certain scheduled caste by their clothing, job, skin color, home, food, or simply their deferential manner; in the U.S. one can similarly tell the difference between class in much the same way. A Wall Street banker is easily discernable from the janitor in her building, and factory workers don't generally mix with doctors or lawyers. Like most forms of discrimination and apartheid, it is most prevalent among those with lower incomes and education levels and far more common in rural areas than urban. To an educated, middle class tech worker in Bangalore or Chennai, caste would likely be irrelevant. In other circumstances, people are still killed over it.

Vishal Sharma, eighteen, and Sonu Singh, seventeen, were publicly hanged to death by their families in November 2001 for planning an inter-caste marriage, as hundreds of spectators looked on.[xiii] Five years later, a sixteen-year-old Dalit girl who had been raped refused to withdraw the charges against her attacker. In retaliation, the accused poured kerosene on her and set her on fire while she slept.[xiv] The Human Rights Watch conducted an extensive investigation in 2006 into ongoing caste discrimination and violence, reporting to the UN Committee on the Elimination of Racial Discrimination that such divisions and abuse based on caste amounted to a "hidden apartheid."[xv] The report charged that Dalit children faced exclusion, discrimination and abuse in schools from both fellow students and teachers;[xvi] and documented the particular vulnerability of these children when employed in child labor and living with HIV/AIDS.[xvii] Children from the scheduled castes have lower school enrollment and literacy rates, and higher dropout rates, than other children.

Although I had heard stories from Caroline of incidents such as private doctors refusing to treat our kids, for the first time I was seeing, and feeling, this discrimination first-hand. Fellow volunteer Kathleen felt it, too. "I thought, 'Oh my God, how could they be so disgusted with these lovely children?'" she said to me later. "But there it was. Inside the safe walls of the ashram, I did not realize it."

The children seemed oblivious to the stares and what they meant, however. For this I was glad.

* * *

We headed to the botanical gardens across the lake. They were beautiful, large expanses of lily and flower-covered water surrounded by lush trees and vegetation. At our picnic spot, some of the staff had arrived early and prepared lunch; black pots bubbled with the familiar vegetables and dal over a huge fire they had built. We ate on blankets spread on a bluff under the trees with the birds singing overhead. After lunch the kids wasted no time jumping on the playground equipment, slides and swings and a merry-go-round.

The volunteers spread out on the blankets, feeling sleepy from the food and heat. I was drowsy but resisted a nap, not wanting to miss one of these last moments. Instead I wrote in my journal. After a while some of the children tired of the playground and invaded our blankets. Santosh plopped down and grinned at me, his hair and shirt damp with sweat. He peered over my shoulder at what I was writing, and I poked him gently in the chest with my pen.

"It's about *you*," I said.

I turned the page over and drew four intersecting lines, a grid, on the blank side. "Do you know how to play tic-tac-toe?"

Santosh shook his head, so I demonstrated, marking an X and then an O, showing how the goal was three in a row. Excited by the new game, he quickly caught on. I drew another grid and we traded the pen back and forth. I beat him several times as he learned the game and then suddenly he won a round. His face gleamed. Other boys gathered in an interested circle around us. Bikram had to play me, then Umesh. More pens were found and soon they were challenging each other. Daina came to sit beside me, oblivious to the boys, and took my hand.

I had been waiting all week to see which of the unsponsored children would develop a special bond with me. Daina was one of the newer children. She had been at the orphanage for seven months. Her father had abandoned the family the previous summer, his whereabouts unknown. Left alone with a child, Daina's mother, an illiterate day laborer, had no one to look after the little girl while she worked. In any case, alone she was unable to provide for the both of them. I could only imagine it must have been with a grieving heart that she brought her daughter to Papa's home, three days before the girl's fifth birthday.

Daina smiled up at me, crowding close to my legs in her ruffled pink dress with the sash untied. Her short bangs blew across her forehead in the breeze and her little pixie face radiated happiness as she squeezed my hand between both of hers. The life of hardships she must have had wasn't visible in her face. I knew I could never replace her missing mother, and I wouldn't have tried. Perhaps one day Daina's mother would also receive some small assistance that would raise her out of abject poverty and enable her to keep her family together. But until then, at least I could be a person in her life who cared about her, who knew she was special and could form some sort of relationship with her. I only wanted Daina to know she was someone to somebody.

Squeezing her hand back, I asked if she'd like me to be her sponsor. She dropped her head and smiled self-consciously. I knew it was a yes.

More blankets were spread out and all the children gathered. Papa placed a folding chair at the front of our seated group and announced that, except for Caroline and a few who were continuing on to the tsunami village in South India, this was the volunteers' last day. It was a bittersweet moment, and I saw tears in the eyes of many – children and adults alike. Srabani pulled up the hem of her dress to wipe under an eye and Daina looked quickly over at me, her new sponsor. I held Santosh's hand as Papa thanked us all for being here this week and asked us to come back – not in 2006, but later in 2005! He led the children in a cheer: "2005! 2005!" they cried, clapping their hands. Caroline told them to study hard, especially their English.

Then Papa began our final prayer together. "Om...om..." As the song ended with "shanti, shanti, shanti," I thought of the meaning of the words I had been taught. Peace to the world, peace to the universe, peace to every heart. I had come expecting this to be a sad place, an emotionally wrenching experience with these parentless young people. But those expectations had been turned on their head. Yes, there were stories behind each one of these children – many of them painful and tragic. Stories of death, abandonment, abuse, poverty. They all had a past. Yet Papa and his family had made these kids their own in a community of sharing and acceptance. They were poor in wealth but not in spirit; limited in resources but not in joy and laughter. An interior

peace shown from inside them which was unknown –
unsought even – by most people rich in resources.

I looked around at the clear, innocent faces and
memorized them; already missing this place and these
people who had taken up permanent residence in my heart.
Whatever I might be leaving behind seemed such a small
thing, almost selfish, because the return I had gotten was far
greater. Here I was always awash in an outpouring of the
innocent, true, powerful love they gave so easily and
unconditionally, for nothing more than showing up. They
broke my heart and made it whole again all at the same
time.

---

xi PBS, "Escape From Affluenza," September 1997,
http://www.pbs.org/kcts/affluenza/escape/.
xii <u>Affluenza: The All-Consuming Epidemic</u> by John De Graaf,
David Wann and Thomas H. Naylor, Berrett-Koehler Publishers,
August 2002.
xiii <u>Being Indian</u>, by Pavan K. Varma, published by Penguin
Books, 2004.
xiv ZeeNews.com, "Dalit Girl Burnt to Death by Man Accused of
Rape," Nov. 23, 2006.
xv Human Rights Watch. Hidden Apartheid: Caste Discrimination
against India's "Untouchables." 2006.
xvi Human Rights Watch. Hidden Apartheid: Caste
Discrimination against India's "Untouchables," page 94. 2006.
xvii Human Rights Watch. Hidden Apartheid: Caste
Discrimination against India's "Untouchables," page 18. 2006.

"An individual has not started living until he can rise above
the narrow confines of his individualistic concerns to the
broader concerns of all humanity."

– *Martin Luther King, Jr.*

How the Other Half Lives

Back home, I found myself missing India every day. The world I had previously inhabited seemed so quiet and bland when I returned to it. Food was tasteless in my mouth, jeans and t-shirts a dull plateau against the rich Technicolor I had just left. The streets were quiet, the sidewalks empty; people kept their distance. It seemed somehow lacking without the constant in-your-face life of India. The incredible, rich, exotic beauty was side by side with poverty and chaos and need. I missed the beauty, but I also missed those reminders that there existed a world outside the sheltered one which is the only world so many of us know, therefore enabling us to believe that life is such for everyone. It was a world in which I felt blessed in ways far more than I had ever earned.

The middle class and wealthy enjoy a life of relative ease and amenity – just as true in India as in the U.S. – while so many more who barely manage to survive endure so much. Before my journey it had been far too easy in my comfortable existence to accept this life of plenty as one I was somehow entitled to, somehow deserved. But the truth was I had done nothing to deserve my incredible lot in life; by far it was a lottery of birth, of geography. I wouldn't allow myself to wear blinders against that truth; nor the simple, unfair reality that these children had likewise done nothing to deserve the lot that was theirs. They were as deserving, as bright and lovely and hopeful, as any other child who had a home, love, and opportunities.

Poverty threatens children's very survival. It increases their vulnerability not only to loss of parents and home, but also to malnutrition, disease, illiteracy, discrimination, labor and trafficking. More than two million children die every year from diseases virtually eradicated in industrialized countries, and many more are orphaned by them.[xi] A poor child in India is three times as likely to die before his fifth birthday as a rich child.

In their 2006 State of the World's Children report, UNICEF stated, "Millions of children make their way through life impoverished, abandoned, uneducated, malnourished, discriminated against, neglected and vulnerable. Whether they live in urban centers or rural outposts, they risk missing out on their childhood – excluded from essential services such as hospitals and schools, lacking the protection of family and community, often at risk of exploitation and abuse."[xii]

The root causes of exclusion were identified in the report as: poverty, weak governance, armed conflict and

HIV/AIDS, naming these as among the greatest threats to childhood today.[xx]

Not only do children suffer damage from which they may never fully recover, but they are at much higher risk of being exploited, neglected, trafficked or abused. The repercussions are felt beyond individual children. Entire countries struggle when citizens are poorly educated or ravaged by disease, resulting in stunted economic development and leaving nations vulnerable to instability and even armed conflict.[xxi] This creates a vicious cycle which deepens and perpetuates poverty, generating a ripple that affects other countries and eventually spills over to the entire global village.

UNICEF clearly defined what it means to be an invisible child. Invisible children lack an environment that protects them from violence, abuse and exploitation; they go without basic necessities such as adequate food, health care and schooling. They are subject to rights violations – particularly child protection abuses and state neglect. These factors often overlap and intertwine, "each exacerbating the next until, at the extremes, some excluded children are made invisible – denied their rights, physically unseen in their communities, unable to attend school and obscured from official view through absence from statistics, policies and programmes."[xxii]

Many are invisible before they even put a footprint upon the earth. Less than half of all births in India are registered; in the rural areas, three out of four children born are not registered. Although this may seem a mere

formality, the repercussions can be enormous. Unregistered
children are not recognized in official statistics and may be
denied access to fundamental rights such as schools and
hospitals. Later in life, they are unable to open a bank
account, vote, inherit land, obtain a passport or even prove
their own nationality.[xxiii] Children like Caroline's Sibani,
found abandoned in the bushes when she was only days
old. Without a name, a birth certificate or known parents,
Sibani officially had no identity. In this way such children
are denied even a legal existence.

For millions of children, daily life is simply a struggle
to survive. Before going to India I had assumed that most of
those living at The Miracle Foundation home were orphans
in the truest sense of its definition – their parents had died.
But hearing their stories, reading case reports and talking
with Caroline, I began to realize that most of them had been
orphaned due to poverty rather than death. Perhaps one
parent had died, and the other could not afford to feed the
family alone. In other cases parents had abandoned their
families – again the root cause most often being poverty. In
this world employment was hard to come by, clean water
might require a walk of several miles, immunizations were
virtually unheard of and parents and children alike
routinely died from simple, treatable maladies.

What these children learn, at far too young an age, is
that seismic change is not the only earth-shattering kind.
Sometimes life is altered in an instant, the ground opening
up underneath and swallowing everything known and safe.
More common, though, in fact happening every day to

millions of children, is the gradual type of change. It happens slowly and quietly, so that they don't even realize their world has become an entirely different place until they're past it, deep in a new world. It might have been a difficult life before, one in which food and water were far from plentiful, education and medical care even more rare; yet it was a world in which the very worst was still unknown.

There are tens of thousands of children living on that precipice of the very worst every day. Babies like Sibani who are discarded at birth, or toddlers like Santosh who had been when abandoned by his father after his mother's death. In the rural towns and villages around the orphanage, I saw these potential disasters in the making, children one small catastrophe away from life on the streets.

Going to the ashram each day, we had driven along a river just outside Cuttack where some of the poorest people lived. Baxter, one of the volunteers who was a producer of film, video and interactive digital media, wanted to take some footage for a documentary he was making about The Miracle Foundation. So one afternoon he, Matt, Kathleen and I had stopped at a spot we had driven past every day.

Rohit, the driver, pulled to the side of the road and we got out of the car. Immediately life in the vicinity came to a halt. Everyone stopped what they were doing to stare. Bicyclists even stopped their journeys mid-pedal, almost falling over as they gawked at us. Matt began taking still shots as Baxter set up his camera on its tripod. I was a little more reticent and hovered by the car with Kathleen, feeling self-conscious from the attention we created.

The community was a shantytown, really. Houses consisted of corrugated tin huts propped up precariously, or nothing more than palm leaves or plastic stretched between trees. For the houses that had doorways, blankets were the doors. People sold what they could along the road, repaired bicycles and mopeds, or begged. Toddlers ran naked and barefoot down the side of the dirt road that was lined with an unbelievable amount of trash. Along the expanse of ground beyond them were piles of burning rubbish; kids picked through it even as it blazed. Girls of ten or twelve acted as surrogate parents, swinging babies on their hips or tied to their backs. Women walked by with firewood, water or loads of bricks balanced atop their heads. They washed clothes and dishes in the filthy river while their children bathed alongside them. The dust was on everything, an incessant presence. The air smelled like rancid trash, sweat and cow dung.

A small crowd of men gathered around Baxter's equipment. Their curiosity couldn't have been greater if a UFO had landed in their midst. As he fumbled in front of the camera, the men quickly crouched down to peek through the viewfinder as if it gave them a whole new vision of their world.

With the cameras out bystanders began to venture a little closer. The people were polite, but greatly intrigued. Kathleen and I tentatively started to take a few pictures. Soon the villagers' curiosity overcame their reserve and they moved closer. A woman in a threadbare purple sari and her three children approached me uncertainly. I indicated that I'd like to take a photo and she nodded. I snapped it and then turned the camera around to show the kids their picture on the digital screen.

That did it – one thing I have found is that people almost everywhere, young and old, love to have their picture taken; even more, they love to see themselves in the photo. Digital photography was a godsend in making friends with strangers, even if you didn't speak the same language. Instantly a dozen more kids were around, jumping in front of us and hamming it up for the cameras. One girl of about thirteen held her small brown and white dog in front of my lens. The adults too followed after a bit. I took photo after photo, showing them to the crowd. The adults looked away with embarrassment, while the kids chortled and thumped each other on the back.

I knew that Santosh and Daina, in fact most all the kids in the orphanage, had come from surrounding communities just like this one. Maybe some had even once lived along this river. The people in this village lived and they died without leaving even a ripple on the surface. Virtually everything outside mere existence is irrelevant. The faces I photographed stayed with me long after we had driven away.

* * *

We went farther afield as well, to much more remote rural communities. Papa took us to the Christian Children's

Fund village where he first met Caroline on Mother's Day 2000. CCF had since pulled out, but the village remained, as timeless as the plains and hills that surrounded it. We rode for about an hour, driving through ever smaller towns until all signs of development were left behind and we entered true country. The landscape was truly lovely, rice fields and palm trees with low clouds hugging the mountains against the horizon.

The state of Orissa has abundant natural resources – fertile rivers, regular rainfall, lush forests and wildlife sanctuaries, mineral resources and a large coastline, although there is only one port of any significance. Home to thirty-two million people, its rich cultural history and historical sites date back to the Stone Age. Scholars from long-ago Greece, China and Persia studied at its ancient universities, some of the oldest discovered academic ruins in the world. Known as the "Land of Temples," its centuries-old legacy includes classical music and dance forms, as well as the exquisite temples. Thousands of visitors flock to Puri and the Sun Temples of Konark each year; the design of world famous Angkor Wat in Cambodia has Orissan roots.[xxiv]

Despite its opulent heritage, today Orissa is one of the poorest places in India. A highly agricultural state, nearly nine out of ten citizens live in rural villages, and one-third of those own no land of their own. They are largely Dalits, the lower castes. The unemployment rate for Dalits and tribal groups is double that of non Dalits or tribals.[xxv] Although agriculture makes up eighty percent of the

workforce it constitutes only twenty percent of the GDP
(gross domestic product),[xxvi] figures which help illuminate
the vast income differences between farming and industrial
work. In spite of the phenomenal economic growth rate
happening in urban India since 1991, rural growth has
remained stagnant and the agricultural sector weak.[xxvii] In
the summer of 2004, hundreds of marginalized farmers
trapped in debt committed suicide within a six week period,
bringing the total to-date number of farmer suicides in India
to nearly ten thousand.[xxviii]

Gandhi once said, "India lives in the villages." If that is
so, they are the ones increasingly being left behind in the
country's new success story. Orissa receives the lowest per-
capita investment from the government of any state. Only
twenty percent of its roads are paved; infrastructure and
education lag behind much of the rest of the country.[xxix] The
bucolic image of peaceful village life makes it easy for many
of the elite, often far removed in urban power hubs, to
remain blind to the economic and social injustice that is by
far rural India's bigger reality.

The farther into the country we drove, the difference in
dress of the people became more pronounced. Far from the
vibrantly colored silks of the city, these women wore tired
and faded cotton saris of dull and indeterminable color, the
edges ragged. Their ears, wrists and ankles were
conspicuously missing the flashy, jangling jewelry I had
grown accustomed to seeing on most women. Men had
sarong-like wraps tied about their hips; many wore them on
their heads as well. We passed dozens of women walking

alongside the dirt road with huge loads of branches balanced atop their heads, and men cutting stone and brick from the red earth under the scorching midday sun – both backbreaking endeavors.

When we reached the village children of all ages crowded around to inspect the vehicle, peering in the windows. "How often does a car come here?" I asked Papa.

"Perhaps one time every month," he replied.

An elderly woman draped in a simple green sari laid a small wooden platform on the ground in front of us, then held her palms together in front of her chest. "Namaste," she said.

"Namaste," I echoed with the same gesture.

She knelt before the platform with a bowl of water tinted with yellow powder. One by one, we removed our shoes and stood on the wooden riser, where the woman washed our feet and then touched her fingers to her forehead in blessing. As we stepped down from the platform a teenage girl sprinkled a handful of rice and fresh white flowers over our heads.

The village consisted of a number of thatched huts and small houses constructed of concrete or the bricks we saw being carved from the rock of the surrounding hillsides. There was no plumbing, no electricity. Windows were one or two small holes in the walls. The heat that day was oppressive, almost unbearable, and I could not imagine how it must have felt inside those houses even at night. The typical rural home is one hundred-fifty to two hundred square feet for an entire family, providing an average living space slightly larger than a full-size bed per person. Only nineteen percent of rural Indians live in adequate housing, with toilets in just thirteen percent. Respiratory problems and chronic tuberculosis are common due to the poor sanitation and inadequate ventilation, especially when cooking is done inside the house where smoke fumes become trapped.[xxx]

Two out of three people in Orissa do not have access to safe, clean drinking water.[xxxi] I watched as several women squatted on the low stone wall of a community well and lowered their heavy metal pots into the water with a rope. I wondered if the still water could be breeding grounds for mosquitoes. The previous morning I had read in the newspaper that Orissa was the malaria capital of India, as I swallowed my anti-malarial pills brought from home.

Papa greeted the community leaders while several yards away other residents grouped and stared at us. I saw faces peering out of windows and doorways, surreptitiously studying these visiting strangers. The children were less reticent, crowding up to us and elbowing each other with grins when we said hello or smiled at them. Sodas were brought, a selection that included Sprite, an orange drink and the Indian cola called "Thums Up", which tasted like salty Tab. The purchase of eleven sodas in this tiny community, far removed from any town and where most residents lived on less than a dollar a day, was not insignificant. I was struck by the kindness with which we were received; the grace and nobility in which lives were lived despite such conditions.

Everyone was barefoot, and the calloused soles of their feet were thick and weathered. A stooped, shriveled man weighing all of perhaps ninety pounds walked over with a smoothed tree-branch cane. A younger man by his side explained in English that this was the village elder. The dark, leathery face lined with deep crevices suggested that the old man was at least eighty, but the translator revealed him to be fifty-seven.

Caroline had brought a personal donation for the village and we were led to the community center for its presentation. Far less grand than the name suggested, the community center was a tiny dwelling of about twelve feet by five, with a dirt floor and two openings in the stone for windows. A small building nearby, perhaps four feet by seven, served as a village market of sorts; meat and fresh foods hung in bags from the ceiling to prevent animals from getting to them. In most places either structure would be considered fit only for livestock. The center was completely empty except for a couple of stone benches which we sat on while the entire rest of the village crowded outside the doorway and jostled each other for the best viewing of us inside.

The donation being made was a monetary bequest to improve and expand this community center, which was the heart of village life. There was much pomp and circumstance surrounding the gift. Papa selected three villagers to do the work on the building and they were brought forward for a prayer and a blessing. Papa made a speech, something I suspected that, for all his humility, he loved to do whenever there was a crowd. Because he spoke in Oriyan I could not understand, so I took photos of the children until he wound down.

But it wasn't finished there. A contract was needed. A piece of paper was found, a pen, and Papa labored over just the right words, flowery formal language he wrote painstakingly on the paper. The ten of us sat inside the community center with Papa, waiting for the ritual to be concluded. When the contract was finished it was sent out, and still we waited. Ten minutes passed, then twenty, but no one moved.

I found myself musing about leisure time, recreation, entertainment. Between trying to eke out some form of a living and taking care of their homes and children, I was certain that most of these people worked from far before dawn until night. There were no toys, no movies, no sports equipment or pets here. Leisure time was an indulgence, the province of the well-to-do, and just one more indicator of the abyss of difference between the haves and the have-nots of this world. To have recreational time, to be able to enjoy entertainment, was a luxury for those with plenty.

The people remained glued in the doorway, enjoying the show. The waiting continued. At long last, the paper came back and I discovered what had taken so long – it had been signed by every one of the adult villagers. A prayer was sung over the finished contract. "Take a snap!" Papa demanded as the money changed hands. We left the center and headed back to the cars, everyone trailing in excitement. Papa began a chant.

"Long live Caroline!" he shouted, then repeated it.
Soon many of the villagers had taken up the chant. "Long
live Caroline!"

Caroline shook her head, waved off their exaltations.
She was truly bothered, I could see, by being perceived or
treated as some white Western "rescuer" who swooped in
and threw cash like a dilettante. Her face reddened in
mortification as she tried to quiet Papa.

It hit home to me just how much a small amount of
money meant here, how greatly lives could be changed with
such a little bit that I would take for granted and never even
miss. I wondered how many of the children following me
would be orphaned or abandoned before they were grown
or how many might die themselves? How many of these
little faces were at risk of becoming another Sibani, left in
the bushes? How many parents might succumb to malaria
or tuberculosis, leaving the remaining parent no choice but
to give their children to others so they might have the
possibility of being fed?

While some agricultural incentives and anti-poverty
programs had reduced the number of people living in rural
poverty from sixty-three percent in 1991 to forty-two
percent in 2001, there had been no such sweeping reforms
in the health care system. Maternal and child health remains
one of the biggest issues. Rural infant mortality rates are
almost twice that of urban areas, and maternal mortality
rates are also significantly higher – and rising over the last
decade. Three-fourths of pregnancies occur in females

under age eighteen, and half of all childbirths happen at home with untrained attendants.[xxxii]

For the families in this village, health inequalities only begin with childbirth. More than half the children are malnourished and underweight.[xxxiii] Eighty percent are affected by parasitic worms, and simple diarrheal diseases are the primary cause of early childhood deaths.[xxxiv] While almost all rural medical practitioners handle diarrhea conditions regularly, fewer than one out of three know how to make the oral rehydration solutions to treat it.

Twenty thousand new doctors are trained every year in India, gleaming new hospitals open by the dozens and the pharmaceutical industry is booming, yet little of it reaches these villages. Three-fourths of rural villages have no primary healthcare centers and medicine is unavailable to them.[xxxv] The rural health centers that do exist are significantly understaffed, undersupplied, and underfunded. The doctor to patient ratios are six times lower than in cities; even more alarming, eighty percent of rural general practitioners do not have proper training.[xxxvi] Government doctors spend an average of one minute per patient and prescribe the wrong medicine half the time.[xxxvii]

The continually failing health care infrastructure remains one of the most striking examples of the two faces of India: urban and rural, rich and poor. Not only do these impoverished villagers have little access to quality medical attention, the inadequate system is actually making them poorer. Most people in India – wealthy and poor alike – resort to private, paid health care ranging from local medical doctors to traditional healers. Individual health care spending has become one of the most common causes of poverty in the country, pushing two hundred million more below the poverty line each year. Nearly two-thirds of families like those in this village are spending over half of their meager annual income on health and medical care.[xxxviii]

* * *

Those living in rural areas are more likely to live in poverty than those living in urban areas – except for the urban slums, which are massive in India. Much urban poverty is a direct result of rural citizens migrating to cities to try and find work. UNICEF reports that in cities the world over, "the most impoverished citizens live in slums, tenements and shanty towns, areas which are geographically separate from the most affluent." These slums are severely lacking in essential services such as decent housing, sanitation and access to clean, safe water.[xxxix] Their citizens are pushed to the very margins of society, existing in the smallest sliver of space possible.

In America in the late 19th and early 20th centuries, New York was a city in which three-fourths of the population lived in ghettos of appalling conditions. Far from the huge middle class the United States has today, there existed a much starker chasm between two social classes – the wealthy and the poor. The major cities of India today can arguably be compared to New York of a hundred years ago; in fact many of its social problems mirror the same trajectory of the United States' history in the last century.

Gender discrimination, classism and racism, the taboo of unwed pregnancy and hidden nature of sex and sex education – these are all social chasms that still exist in the United States in a far milder extent, but that fifty or a hundred years ago were just as widespread as they are today in India.

The big change for the U.S. came with the Industrial Revolution. As this period of time brought the country huge growth in terms of economy, trade, prosperity and wealth, our social stratifications of race, class and gender began to shift as well. This same thing is happening in India today, only it is the Tech Revolution instead of the Industrial Revolution driving it. And this revolution is light-years faster in advancement. Where the Industrial Revolution created slow and steady change over fifty years, the Tech Revolution is forcing the same types of social upheaval in India in a much faster time period.

In most ways a sixty year old nation since its independence and unification, India's explosion onto the global economy in 1991 brought an influx of new wealth. Its emergence on the international markets with leading industries such as technology, pharmaceuticals and manufacturing have put it squarely in the center of global importance, with an astounding annual growth rate of over nine percent.[xl] The country has more billionaires than the United Kingdom or Japan[xli] and is home to the fastest growing middle class in history, whose numbers are more than the entire population of the United States. They are buying nearly a million cars per year, seven million motorcycles, and in 2006 there were eighty-two million new mobile phone subscriptions.[xlii] This trend was illustrated perfectly in a woman I saw once, who was pulled over on the side of the road outside a small town. Dressed in a traditional sari, she sat on her moped in the middle of nowhere, chatting on her cell phone. India has emerged as the world's fastest growing wealth creator, thanks to a buoyant stock market and higher earnings.[xliii]

Yet even as the urban elite are prospering, new poverties are being created in a country where everything and nothing is changing. Hundreds of millions are shut off from the boom, living completely outside the affluence it brings. Eighty percent of the population lives on less than two dollars a day and only thirty-three percent have access to sanitation.[xliv] Some are merely left out of this shimmering new India while others are actively dislodged by it.

Mumbai, Delhi and Calcutta are all home to massive, sprawling slums in which a large portion of their citizens live. As in other countries with great wealth disparities, many of India's elite embrace its greatly increasing income, economic prosperity, and emerging superpower status while choosing to pretend they do not see how the other half lives. Indian academics and government watchdog groups warn that the current economic growth cannot be sustained unless those in power spread its benefits to the wider population and invest much more heavily in basic infrastructure such as healthcare, water, electricity and education.[xlv]

In Mumbai I came face to face with India's tale of two cities. One is on the streets, right up front – the beggars, the pavement dwellers, the street children who pick through litter for recyclables when they should be laughing on a playground. It's noisy, in your face, assaulting. The other India is cocooned behind all this, tucked away from it. This India is one of quiet, air conditioning, service and amenities; middle and upper class people living their lives much as those with means live their lives anywhere. Doctors, professors, engineers, computer programmers. They live in beautiful gated homes or modern flats and spend evenings in premier restaurants and hip, trendy nightclubs with loud techno music and drinks that cost what they would in New York or London.

A notion can permeate that the whole of the country is its elite – five percent of the population – and the rest are the problem. Mostly, these two Indias exist separately from each other, as if each half is unaware of the other side's existence. Sometimes, however, they clash, happening more and more every day in social upheaval that demands change, reform and equality.

In the very center of Mumbai sits an area called Dharavi, widely known as the largest slum in Asia.[xlvi] After visiting Dharavi, British journalist Dan McDougall wrote, "If India's biggest city is seen by economists as its great hope, Mumbai also embodies most of the country's staggering problems. The obstacles hampering India's progress – poor infrastructure, weak government, searing inequality, corruption and crime – converge in Mumbai like nowhere else. Here, where £4m penthouses look over filthy slums, India's class divide is at its starkest."[xlvii]

A local tour operator named Deepa Krishnan learned I was writing a book about India and offered to show me Dharavi. Deepa donates approximately one-third of the profits from her tour company Mumbai Magic to an organization called Akanksha, which provides education and mentoring for children living in slum communities. She is also somewhat of an expert on Dharavi.

Our meeting point was a spot that overlooked Dhobi Ghat, the world's largest outdoor laundry. Spread below me were hundreds of concrete wash bins formed into the ground, filled with murky water. At most of them men were beating clothes against the stone or rubbing them with soap. In between and along the wash pools, thousands of pieces of clothing and laundry hung from lines, stretching easily a quarter of a mile. More covered the roofs of the buildings. Workers stood at tables ironing sarees and jeans with old-fashioned coal irons, while others folded them.

Deepa's car pulled up and she got out and introduced herself. Petite and plump, she was a ball of compacted energy. Her hair was cut in a short, fashionable style and she wore a gorgeous navy blue silk sari patterned with gold and burgundy leaves and flowers. She had on simple jewelry – large pearls dotted each ear, a watch was on her left wrist and one thick gold bangle encircled her right.

We stood looking over Dhobi Ghat. In Hindi, a "dhobi" is a traditional laundryman – and in Dhobi Ghat more than two hundred dhobis work, some of them third or fourth generation. More than half a million items of clothing are washed there every day.[xlviii] The operation looked incredibly organized, yet there was simply so much laundry I could not imagine how it was all kept track of.

As we drove away through the bustling streets of Mumbai, Deepa gave me a history lesson on Dharavi. In the early days of the city the land on which it sits was a swamp, later filled in so it could be utilized as a sort of human dumping ground on which to shove the poor of booming Mumbai. As the city sprawled outward, however, its inexorable and immense growth grew to encompass Dharavi.

"What is the population?" I asked.

"Exact figures are difficult," Deepa said, "but it's estimated that close to a million people live in Dharavi." I later substantiated her figure with numerous magazine and newspaper articles that have been written about the infamous slum, including National Geographic, Time Magazine Asia and The Guardian.

One of the official indicators of a slum, along with overcrowding, lack of water and sanitation, and non-durable housing structures, is the percentage of residents living in illegal housing. Not only is most of Dharavi's housing illegal, but so is ninety percent of its commercial enterprises. This illegal status often deprives residents of public services. Women might walk for miles to get potable water, and there is only one proper toilet with plumbing for every fifteen hundred residents – a staggering statistic I could not wrap my head around.[xlix] Children living in such

poor conditions are more likely to die from pneumonia,
diarrhea, malaria, measles or HIV/AIDS than those living in
a non-slum area, and are more vulnerable to respiratory
illnesses and other infectious diseases.[1] There is no hospital
in Dharavi; cholera, typhoid and malaria are common. Half
of Mumbai's nineteen million citizens live in such an urban
slum.

Yet Dharavi was not a slum in the way I had imagined
– not a ghetto. Our car turned from a major, four-lane
avenue onto a smaller street lined with beauty shops and
stores selling tires, bangles or dosas and other snacks.
Lottery tickets and fresh vegetables were sold side by side.
Uniformed schoolchildren walked along the road holding
hands or swinging backpacks.

"We are here," announced Deepa. "You see the
children; almost every child attends school. Oh, there is the
police station. It is the only one in Dharavi."

"Only one police station for a million people?"

"But there is very little crime here, you see," Deepa
assured me.

It looked and felt much more like a village, not a place
right in the middle of the huge, sprawling city of Mumbai.
In fact it reminded me very much of Cuttack, except for the
soaring luxury high-rise buildings looking down over its
teeming five hundred acres. Turning off the main road we
encountered a web of tight lanes that twisted in and out of
each other like a maze. The peeling and stained buildings
rose on either side of the car, often only inches away. People
flattened themselves against the walls or steered their

bicycles into doorways to allow us passage. We carefully wove around cows and mules or oxen pulling wooden carts.

My friend Dita, an Indian-American whose family moved from Bangalore to Houston when she was ten, once observed that wealth requires space. Nowhere was this more apparent than a place like Dharavi. The residents here seemed to have no privacy, no moments of solitude or sanctuary. They lived virtually on top of one another. In the midst of the bustle, food was cooked, tea was made. Children were bathed and fed and sent off to school.

Hindu temples stood yards away from mosques. Around one corner wooden pens filled with live chickens and lambs lined the streets. "This is the Muslim section," Deepa said. "Oh, there is the movie theater!" She pointed toward the second floor of a narrow building as we rounded another corner. "Movies are a very popular past-time."

We headed down the next lane, but were immediately confronted by a large truck coming right at us. There was clearly no room for both vehicles; I was amazed just at the sight of the truck, as I would have been sure it would not fit in this alley. Our driver put the car in reverse and steered back out the way we had come.

"Should we get out here and walk?" Deepa suggested.

We attracted attention at once, the grubby foreigner and the fancy Indian lady in her rich attire. The children of Dharavi tailed us like sleuths as we wound through the pathways. A girl of about nine in a sky blue skirt posed for me, clasping her hands together nervously and looking at her mother instead of the camera. She followed me as we walked on.

"Hello, what's your name?" I asked. She only smiled and said nothing. None of the children seemed to speak English except two teenage boys who fell into stride next to me.

"Where from?" they wanted to know. "England?"

"United States," I said.

"America!" the first boy exclaimed. "You America?"

"Yes," I smiled, and the second boy punched him in the arm victoriously. I wondered if they had discussed where I might be from before approaching me. Before we could talk further they darted off, no more time to spare for this silliness.

We came out into an open space and watched women making papadam, a thin crispy bread with bits of pepper in it. Squatting along the ground in the shade, they rolled the balls of meal out on little ceramic plates with thin wooden or metal rolling pins. Then, the tortilla-like rounds were placed on wicker baskets turned upside down beside them to crisp in the sun. Finished papadam wafers were stored in clear plastic bags for selling. Dozens of women performed this task, gossiping amongst themselves while their toddlers hopped around them.

The making of papadam depended on the sun for baking. "In the three monsoon months starting July, these households have to look for other sources of income," said Deepa. She led the way down another lane, through a door and then up a steep fold-down ladder like I had in my attic. A rope hung down from the ceiling rafters to help the ascent into the tiny clothing workroom we entered. A man greeted Deepa warmly while other men worked at sewing machines, making shirts in assembly-line fashion. One did the cutting, another sewed the sleeves, a third the collar, and on down the line to the finished product. The man in charge held up a beautiful completed shirt, which Deepa said would sell wholesale to a retail store buyer for fifteen rupees, about thirty-five cents.

Another section of the neighborhood was dedicated entirely to a pottery industry. "There is a simple logic in the layout," said Deepa. "At the front of the house, on the roadside, the pots are sold. If you enter the front door, you see the potter's home. Pass through the kitchen, and you're in a little workshop, where pots are fashioned."

We walked back and watched a woman mix clay for her husband as he sat at the potter's wheel, skillfully and intently forming the perfect urn out of a muddy brown lump. Afterward Deepa confessed, playfully like a mischievous child, "I wanted to poke a finger in it, and watch the mud groove around my finger." The potter scooped the finished product away from the wheel in one smooth movement and started another.

"Beyond this workshop is a common open area, where you can see the kilns where the pots are baked." Deepa led me down the alley lined with the kilns, their smoke permeating the air and creating a stifling heat in the already ninety-five degree day. Up and down these lanes sat thousands of clay pots and bowls of all shapes and sizes. "Men, women, children – everyone does a part of the work," Deepa explained. "Water has to be fetched and carried, the clay mixed to form the right consistency, and finished pots and pans loaded into trucks." We passed an elderly, stooped woman laboriously carrying a load of pots on her head to a van to be transported for sale.

Industry and entrepreneurship abounded as we wandered through Dharavi. Very few people were idle. Entire cottage industries thrived: weaving, food, clothing manufacturing, pottery. Small business owners worked hard at production, and all around me was the buzz of things happening.

One of Dharavi's largest industries is recycling. Eighty percent of the waste from Mumbai's nineteen million citizens is recycled there, employing almost ten thousand people including children. These small workers collect and haul plastic, glass, cardboard, wire hangers, pens, batteries, computer parts, soap – virtually anything that can be turned into something new with useful life. Nothing is considered garbage. The revenue this generates is staggering – economists estimate it to be a nearly $1.5 *billion* a year business.[li] It surely must be one of the most successful recycling enterprises in the world. The resulting income is well above agricultural wages, an opportunity which draws many rural workers to cities like Mumbai.

But the huge industry exacts its toll on Dharavi. Industrial waste and sludge from batteries or car parts are washed off from the recyclable items and into the streets and drains, mixing with human waste and discards from the butchering done at the chicken and mutton stalls.

To me, this place dispelled the myth that poverty is due to laziness, that the poor somehow deserve their lot in life because they are stupid or apathetic or otherwise lacking in some important character trait that the successful possess. Dharavi was a resounding rebuttal to that belief. I had rarely seen people work so hard in all my life, up to eighteen hours or more each day in demanding physical labor with an unresting pace that few westerners matched. Born into the right mix of circumstances – as the vast majority of "self-made" successes are – the industry-makers here would no doubt be thriving business people with comfortable bank accounts. Instead, by pure chance, they were born into a world with far less access to education and far fewer opportunities to climb onto the next rung of economic prosperity, no matter how smart or hard-working they were.

Deepa understood well the two bewilderingly different Indias – one that is rich and glitzy and safe in their five-star cocoons, and the other that lives a hellish life on the streets, begging and starving. But this left little room for an understanding of a third Mumbai which she presented me: the Mumbai of the hard-working poor. "This is the Mumbai of the aspiring migrant, with his fierce drive for survival, for self-improvement," she said. "The Mumbai of small enterprise. The Mumbai of poor yet strong women, running entire households on the strength of their income from making papads. Every morning, these women put food on the table, braid their daughters' hair, and send them to schools. Dharavi is one place where this third Mumbai is visible. They have hope for the future, you see? This is the Mumbai of dreams."

Despite its spirit and dreams, Dharavi is a community in danger. It sits atop one of the most prime pieces of real estate, its location at the center of one of the world's largest cities enviable. City leaders have unveiled "Vision Mumbai," their plan to create a world-class metropolis by 2013. This plan calls for eyesores full of citizens who don't pay taxes, such as Dharavi, to be eliminated and new, expensive condominiums erected in their places. Residents will be forcibly evicted into government-built housing nearby. Perhaps then, living in massive gray concrete bunkers and dependent on the government in a way they aren't now, the residents will be living in a true slum. And I wonder, what will become of all those children?

xviii USAID website, India Country Profile, http://www.usaid.gov/policy/budget/cbj2005/ane/in.html.
xix UNICEF. The State of the World's Children 2006 – Excluded and Invisible. New York, 2005. Page 1.
xx UNICEF. The State of the World's Children 2006 – Excluded and Invisible. New York, 2005. Pages 11-12.
xxi UNICEF. The State of the World's Children 2006 – Excluded and Invisible. New York, 2005. Page 5-6.
xxii UNICEF. The State of the World's Children 2006 – Excluded and Invisible. New York, 2005. Page 7.
xxiii UNICEF. The State of the World's Children 2006 – Excluded and Invisible. New York, 2005. Pages 36-37.

xxiv Wikipedia, http://en.wikipedia.org/wiki/Orissa.

xxv Human Rights Watch. Hidden Apartheid: Caste Discrimination against India's "Untouchables." 2006.

xxvi Heinz School Review, The H. John Heinz III School of Public Policy and Management, "Healthcare Delivery Systems in Rural India" by Deepti Gudipati, Volume 3, Issue 2, October 13, 2006.

xxvii Wharton University, India Knowledge@Wharton, "India's Rural Poor: Why Housing Isn't Enough to Create Sustainable Communities," August 23, 2007.

xxviii The Times of India, "UN Report Slams India for Farmer Suicides," by Kounteya Sinha, September 24 2006.

xxix Wikipedia, http://en.wikipedia.org/wiki/Orissa.

xxx Wharton University, India Knowledge@Wharton, "India's Rural Poor: Why Housing Isn't Enough to Create Sustainable Communities," August 23, 2007.

xxxi Wikipedia, http://en.wikipedia.org/wiki/Orissa.

xxxii Heinz School Review, The H. John Heinz III School of Public Policy and Management, "Healthcare Delivery Systems in Rural India" by Deepti Gudipati, Volume 3, Issue 2, October 13, 2006.

xxxiii Wharton University, India Knowledge@Wharton, "India's Rural Poor: Why Housing Isn't Enough to Create Sustainable Communities," August 23, 2007.

xxxiv IndianChild.com, "Life Expectancy and Mortality India," http://www.indianchild.com/life_expectany_mortality_india.htm.

xxxv Outlook India, "State of the Nation: Damned Statistics," April 9, 2007.

xxxvi Heinz School Review, The H. John Heinz III School of Public Policy and Management, "Healthcare Delivery Systems in Rural India" by Deepti Gudipati, Volume 3, Issue 2, October 13, 2006.

xxxvii The Times of India, "Our Greatest Achievement: Longer Lives" by Swaminathan S Anklesaria Aiyar, August 19, 2007.

xxxviii Heinz School Review, The H. John Heinz III School of Public Policy and Management, "Healthcare Delivery Systems in Rural India" by Deepti Gudipati, Volume 3, Issue 2, October 13, 2006.

xxxix UNICEF. The State of the World's Children 2006 – Excluded and Invisible. New York, 2005. Page 19.

xl Outlook India, "Elephant Must Remember." April 9, 2007.

xli Forbes Magazine, "The World's Billionaires." March 26, 2007.

xlii International Herald Tribune, "Rising Prosperity Brings New Fears to India" by Anand Giridharadas, Jan. 25, 2007.

xliii Indian Economy: An Overview Nov 13 2006.

xliv Outlook India, "State of the Nation: Damned Statistics," April 9, 2007.

xlv The Christian Science Monitor, "India's Next Test: Spreading Prosperity," by Scott Baldauf, June 26, 2006.

xlvi The Guardian, "Waste Not, Want Not in the £700m Slum" by Dan McDougall, March 4, 2007.

xlvii The Guardian, "Waste Not, Want Not in the £700m Slum" by Dan McDougall, March 4, 2007.

xlviii Frommers, http://www.frommers.com/destinations/mumbai/A21960.html.

xlix The Guardian, "Waste Not, Want Not in the £700m Slum" by Dan McDougall, March 4, 2007.

l United Nations, State of the World's Cities Report 2006-2007, "Urban and Slum Trends in the 21st Century" by Eduardo Lopez Moreno and Rasna Warah.

li The Guardian, "Waste Not, Want Not in the £700m Slum" by Dan McDougall, March 4, 2007.

"How wonderful it is that nobody need wait a single moment before starting to improve the world."

–Anne Frank

The Edge of the River

Back in Austin, The Miracle Foundation began tackling in earnest this double-edged sword – the huge need for care for millions of orphaned and abandoned children, alongside the concurrent crises of poverty that were causing so many to become parentless in the first place. In the beginning, providing for the most basic needs had been the overriding urgency – the children under Papa's care needed beds, clothing, food and medical care. As more people donated to The Miracle Foundation and sponsored children, these immediate needs were slowly met. The focus soon shifted to the bigger picture.

"Imagine a funnel," Caroline told me as I sat across from her in the foundation's office with photos of the children and their framed artwork on the walls all around us. Inside the body of the funnel were the 25.7 million children in India living without parental care. At the top of the funnel, between three and four million more newly orphaned children poured in every single year.[lii] And at the very narrow bottom were those children who found families and homes, the lucky ones who were adopted.

"Do you know how many of those there are?" she asked. "In 2004, it was 3,315 adoptions." Out of twenty-five million children. And of course, many of those millions *had* their own families somewhere, only ones who were too desperately poor to take care of them.

There had been a five-fold increase in domestic Indian adoptions over the fifteen year period between 1988 and 2003, but the figures were still abysmally low next to the overwhelming numbers of children needing homes. Internationally, the numbers were even lower. The Times of India reported that international adoptions had decreased almost forty percent between 2001 and 2003 and that overseas adoptions from India were the lowest in the world.[liii]

Domestically, adoption of non-related children was generally considered risky due to heredity factors – besides genetics and medical conditions, even behavioral problems and unfavorable personality tendencies were thought to be inherited. The practice was not yet socially acceptable among many and remained shrouded in secrecy. Lighter skinned babies were prized, as were males, and so dark complexioned children and girls often languished in institutional homes while years-long waiting lists accrued for the fair-skinned and boys.[liv]

The Hindu Adoption and Maintenance Act allowed only one child of each sex from the same family to be adopted, making the placement of larger sibling groups impossible. The act also allowed only Indian Hindus, Sikhs, Jains and Buddhists to adopt. Indian Christians and Muslims, as well as foreigners, could only apply to be guardians, a relationship which legally ends when the child turns eighteen.[iv] This affects not only inheritance and other legal rights but likely gives children a feeling of not quite being a legitimate part of the family.

Caroline desperately wanted to improve those statistics and make adoption easier, more socially acceptable and safer for children. As she visited different orphanages and began to learn more, a complex and confusing picture of Indian adoption began to crystallize. First, Caroline was told that Indian law required parents to sign a relinquishment form before a child could be adopted. Because the majority of children who ended up in orphanages had been abandoned with no such formal relinquishment, she feared they were not eligible for adoption at all. Instead, they would remain until age seventeen when they would be expected to make lives for themselves with no education, family, or means of support.

Then she discovered that this was not exactly the case; children *could* be adopted without the signed relinquishment by receiving a granted relinquishment by committee, but the process was a bureaucratic nightmare. Corruption and bribes were rampant. Moreover, many children living in group homes or orphanages had not been abandoned at all and were not victims of abuse or neglect; their parents had placed them there because they were too poor to give their children proper food or education. The possibility of children becoming lost forever to families who loved them was all too real.

"Child trafficking was the norm," Caroline said. "I realized that unless I became a participant in this illegal activity, I would not be able to affect the plight of these children." She discussed the problems she faced with a friend and mentor who ran another Austin nonprofit organization serving the homeless. "He said it was not my job alone to save them," she recounted. His words served as a reminder that she needed to connect with others, particularly in India, before she could hope to accomplish what she wanted.

Dr. Manjeet Pardesi, the accountant who had audited the books and helped with tsunami relief, had joined the foundation full-time. He had been so impressed and inspired by the changes he'd witnessed happening before his eyes that he wanted to be a part of it. Leaving his home in Delhi behind and relegating his successful accounting business to part-time status, he had moved his family to Orissa for most of the year to start a new children's home in the town of Rourkela, a few hundred kilometers from Papa's home.

With the help of their staff, Caroline and Manjeet began working with the Indian government to change adoption laws and policy. The Minister of Women and Children Welfare, responsible for policy governing the adoption process and who reports directly to the Prime Minister of India, agreed to meet with them. Manjeet debated about whether Caroline should attend the meeting. "He was afraid that being American, I would hurt our position as an outsider; Caroline said, "and that being me, I would say the wrong thing and offend the minister!"

As they worked on policy changes and regulation enforcement, more children were taken into the homes; more had food and a roof over their heads and went to school. Unlike in many for-profit organizations, the product of such work was immediate, visible and dramatic. It was manifested in one small girl named Sumitra.

Caroline was visiting Manjeet's new orphanage in Rourkela for the first time. On her first day at the home she was dismayed to see how overcrowded the facilities already were. A converted school housed older kids, and a separate building with four tiny rooms and a kitchen was home to twenty-five babies and a half-dozen house mothers. It had gotten so crowded that Manjeet moved five newborn infants and a couple of house mothers to the apartment where he lived with his wife, Pumi, and their three children. Pumi supervised the care of these smallest charges.

The children in the Rourkela home were all new – freshly abandoned or recently orphaned, brought in by relatives or neighbors or police. Their emotions and wounds were raw. These children did not think about the future, where so much seemed unobtainable, but were focused only on the sharpness of the moment. There were no other daydreams or hopes in their lives; there was nothing they wanted other than what they could not have. Everything else was irrelevant. When Caroline picked them up, they almost strangled her by holding on so tightly. When she set them down they began to cry, feeling rejection all over again. Unlike Papa's ashram, the feeling in Rourkela was one of sadness.

After touring the home and seeing how far past capacity it already was, she faced Manjeet. "You have to draw the line," she told him. "You can't keep taking them in, there's no more room. How can we take care of them all?"

"But they found out we are here," he said, referring to the local townspeople. "The children, they just keep coming." He spread his arms wide in a gesture of helplessness.

Originally from Punjab in northwestern India, Manjeet is a Sikh who inherited his passion for human rights from his social worker mother. After obtaining a PhD in banking and then a post-doctorate degree, he started an accounting business that specialized in government audits. He had also run a free elementary school in Punjab for several years before opening the new Miracle Foundation home. Beneath his red turban, his liquid brown eyes gazed at Caroline from behind gold wire-frame glasses. He crossed his arms and stroked his thick mustache and beard thoughtfully as he considered the problem.

But Caroline shook her head decisively. "We need to have standards. We have to be able to care for the children we already have. You've got to stop taking so many in."

Deep into that night – early the next morning, in fact, about two a.m. – Caroline was awakened by a loud knocking at the main entrance. By the time she and some of the house mothers arrived at the front door Manjeet was already there. Standing on the threshold was a police officer, holding a baby.

The child was naked, emaciated with starvation and near death, bones poking her skin up like poles suspending a tent. The look in the eyes of this tiny person, less than a year old, was far beyond infancy. Her dark eyes radiated hopelessness and despair, with the look of someone who had been erased from the inside. The only thing in the world she possessed was the bean strung on a thread around her neck.

The policeman placed the skeletal child into Caroline's arms. The baby's name was Sumitra; she was nine months old but the size of a three month infant. Her mother had died hours earlier from a simple infection. Caroline would later call Sumitra "the saddest human being I have ever seen in my life."

After the officer left the staff tried to feed Sumitra from a bottle, but she kept throwing up the nourishment. They tried massaging her with oil until she relaxed. She was so weak and dehydrated she could not even cry. She simply had no water or energy for tears.

Finally, the exhausted baby took five or six sips of formula and fell asleep. Manjeet just looked at Caroline. That night it was agreed – they would not turn away any child who came to them.

* * *

Sumitra thrived. She spent a few weeks in the hospital, and then under the loving attention of the house mothers began to transform from the weak, emaciated baby who had been brought to the doorstep in the middle of the night. After a few days, she regained the ability to hold up her head. Slowly her flesh filled out as she came closer to eating normal portions of nutritious food. Eventually she even started to smile.

Many of the children taken into Manjeet's home had not even been born yet. A new program had been implemented which assisted unwed pregnant women, providing them with room, board, medical care and properly equipped childbirth facilities. Unwed pregnancy still carries a heavy stigma, and many women who find themselves in this situation are ostracized from their families, considered shameful and unmarriageable. So they often leave their villages, go without pre-natal care, give birth and then, too many times, abandon their babies because they are alone and too poor to care for them. The release that would make these children legally eligible for adoption is never signed.

At the Miracle Foundation home, single, expecting women were welcomed into a safe home and not only cared for, but also taught a skill such as tailoring that would assist them in making new lives for themselves. Many of these women stayed on after the birth of their own children and became house mothers. They could keep their babies, of course, or enter a safe, legal adoption procedure if they felt their child would be better off placed into a loving Indian home. Most chose adoption, having no way to provide for a child and little resources or acceptance of single motherhood in the community. "But *any* girl or woman who is pregnant and needs help is welcome at our orphanage," said Caroline.

Yet to realize any true and lasting effect, the root causes that brought in these women and children like Sumitra needed to be addressed. Simply plucking kids off the streets and giving them food and shelter, or facilitating childbirth and adoption options for women, would do nothing to stem the tide of children pouring into that pool of twenty-five million each year. Caroline began to believe that a bigger vision was possible, and Manjeet was convinced this new model could be replicated over and over. The Miracle Foundation dared to set loftier goals.

What if they could direct their impact to the top of that funnel along with working to ensure the rights of the children already inside it? What if they could somehow help stem the tide of those three or four million children falling through the safety net each year, preventing that funnel from growing exponentially?

"If we can't do that, we're not going to have a prayer at making a lasting change," Caroline bluntly confessed to me. "Children have a right to live with their own families, first and foremost. Placing them in orphanages, even good ones, building more orphanages – these aren't the ultimate answers. We need to find ways to empower the families so that they can remain together, and the children can retain their God-given rights." She offered an Indian proverb to illustrate what she meant.

"A man is standing on the edge of a river when he looks down and sees a baby floating in the water," she said. "He immediately jumps in and saves the child. But he's barely back on shore before he notices another baby in the water. As soon as he rescues that one, here comes another down the stream. He jumps in and out of the water frantically, saving as many babies as he possibly can. But there are so many, he can't possibly reach them all. He's so busy trying to pull the infants out of the river that he never stops to look and see *where* they are coming from – they are being thrown into the water from a bridge upstream. If he would simply look, and stop the man from throwing the babies over the bridge, he could save them all. But, he's too busy looking down at the children in the water all around him."

Organizations and people doing the work such as Caroline, Papa and Manjeet need to keep their gazes high enough to clearly see what is at the root of the problem. And unremittingly, that root cause is poverty. A myriad of other things are tied up in that as well – caste and gender discrimination, illiteracy, sub-par medical care, AIDS – but it's all wrapped up in simple, debilitating poverty. This vision requires a much broader perspective, beyond individual children to entire villages.

"The real way to increase the number of children we can help is to do both – partner with existing orphanages and build new ones for children who don't have a home,"

Caroline explained. The Miracle Foundation began an approach of both starting ideal orphanages – what they called Children's Villages – and partnering with existing orphanages to provide assistance and resources. They also worked with the local communities where the orphanages were located to empower families living in poverty to keep, feed, and educate their children by providing free schooling, meals and immunizations.

"Not a single child should go without food or education," added Manjeet. "If we do this, we can keep increasing capacity always. It is important to own our buildings instead of renting. In this way we can expand our infrastructure and services, and then we can concentrate on the problem areas which are the rural villages."

* * *

Before I left India that March, Mama had invited me into the apartment – two small rooms, really – that comprised the private quarters she and Papa shared. On top of the scarred dresser in the bedroom sat a framed photograph of Mama and Caroline that the older woman pointed to proudly.

"This is Caroline's room; this is Caroline's house," she said. "She is our daughter now." After seating me on a small chair with an orange soda, Mama perched on the bed and smiled at me silently for many long moments. Somehow I felt like her eight year old pupil.

Finally she asked if I enjoyed my stay, and how I liked India. I assured her that I was having an amazing, wonderful experience. She asked about my daughter and I described Chandler's tenth-grade studies and her new school.

Mama nodded. "You bring her?" she asked. "Bring your daughter back to India."

"I would love to," I said. "I promise I will come back, and I will try my best to bring her."

Just then her son, Babu, came into the room wielding a digital camera. In his mid-twenties, Babu lived nearby and worked at a local construction company, and was a frequent presence at the ashram. "Let's take a snap," he suggested.

I sat next to Mama as Babu framed us carefully in the viewfinder and captured the photo. Mama squeezed my hands and continued smiling. "When you come back, your picture will be there too," she said, waving toward the dresser.

* * *

I had no doubt I would return. From my first day with the kids I knew I would be back. But, in the months following my trip, I also thought of taking Chandler and what that would mean – for her, for me, and for my new Indian family in Orissa. At dinner in our safe and cozy house I looked at my daughter, not really a child anymore at fifteen but still in need of a mother, a home. Her long blond hair partially hid her face as her thin shoulders bent over her dinner plate, not noticing my gaze on her. I thought about how it would feel to be unable to feed her, how either of us would bear it if I had to let her go because I lacked the bare necessities required to put a roof over her head and a meal in her stomach.

Then, I wondered how she would possibly survive if that were the case and she was five instead of fifteen, left by herself on the streets in India or in Austin, anywhere. I simply could not imagine it, but I knew many thousands of children were doing just that at the very moment. It was hard for me not to compare the children in the orphanage to a great many children I knew in the United States who had everything, more than they would ever need, and were unsatisfied; whiny, demanding, selfish kids with an astounding sense of entitlement. And it wasn't their fault – those were the values we had taught them.

I didn't want that for my daughter. Already she had a broader sense of the world than I had at her age, and a compassionate nature. Although a typical teenager in many ways, she did carry a certain awareness of politics and social justice. She attended a school that was highly community-service oriented. It required students to complete volunteer service projects and had a class called Global Citizen, which explored the connection between humans and the environment and the role of citizenship in a global perspective. Some students had gone on immersion trips to Senegal and Guatemala.

I yearned to foster that seed in her. I thought, what an incredible blessing it would be for a person to grow into adulthood without the blinders, without the sense that the small corner of the world she knew was the only one there was. When I was a child and even well into adulthood, my view of the world was such a small and narrow one. Beyond the admonition to clear my plate because there were starving children in Cambodia, my family simply had little reference point to the outside world.

Chris, the teenager who had been on the March trip with his mother Diane, had been an exceptional traveler even when his luggage was missing for a week. And, he was a big hit with the kids who loved having an American close to their own ages join in their games of Frisbee and soccer. In fact, it had been Chris's second visit. Dragged somewhat against his will the previous year – he had wanted to go to the beach with friends for Spring Break – when Diane began planning the second trip Chris told her, "Don't even *think* about going without me."

From a travel and adventure perspective as well as a personal and cultural one, I knew Chandler would similarly be enriched by the experience – and I also knew it was a gift she would not take lightly. So, I returned to India exactly one year after my first trip, in March 2006, with Chandler in tow.

The first day I was worried. She was quiet and withdrawn, overwhelmed by the streets and the noises and the heat, uncomfortable with the staring – especially on our train ride, when the first car we boarded was filled with only men who openly inspected our double blue-eyed blondness with fascination. She recoiled on the railway platform when a dozen taxi and rickshaw drivers besieged us the second we stepped off the train, each hawking their services and pushing and wrestling for our bags. Then she went completely still as two small children, a brother and sister, stood in front of us with their fingers touching their mouths, silently begging. Her eyes grew round and wet, and I was afraid she was going to crumple.

I had tried to prepare her for it – the mass of humanity, the filth and smell of garbage, even the beggars; but it was an impossible task, like describing a painting to a blind person. I remembered well the culture shock of arriving in India for the first time. The complete *differentness* of it. I was afraid I had made a huge mistake bringing her. That she hated everything about this crazy, chaotic, often maddening country and was wishing she had never come.

But, all of that was balanced in equal measure with the splendor of intricately carved temples, the majesty of ancient palaces, the smell of incense and curry that wafted on the warm breezes, carried along by soft chanting and the lyrical sing-song of Hindi conversations. There was the warmth and generosity of the people, like the family we met on the train after clumsily hauling our bags out of the car filled with men and into the next one. Immediately a middle-aged woman made room for us, rearranging her family and belongings so we could sit with them. They offered us blankets and shared their food with us, and soon we had learned all about their family – the son in Los Angeles and the architect daughter, the second home in Goa that they were traveling to.

"You are a visitor in our country," the matriarch said, "and it is our duty to take care of you."

That evening in the restaurant where we ate dinner, the fans and night air cooling us, chai and delicious vegetable curry filling our stomachs, Chandler began to perk up. She became talkative again, excitedly recounting our day's adventures as if she had not walked through them in a state of shock. From that moment on India was hers – and she had become India's.

* * *

This time, when I arrived at the airport in Bhubaneswar it was without a large volunteer group. Caroline was in Cuttack already, along with Baxter who had returned from the previous year as well – and was also bringing his child. His son James, a university student in Paris, was meeting his father and happened to be on the same plane from Delhi as Chandler and I.

I immediately saw Papa waiting anxiously on the other side of the baggage claim railing. I ran to hug him over the silver bars and introduced him to Chandler and James. As we put our bags in the car and started the drive to Cuttack I could barely contain my excitement.

"How are the kids, Papa?"

"You will see!"

"How are Daina and Santosh? How's Mama?" I asked.

"You will see!"

"Are they excited?" I persisted. "How is their English?" But Papa only replied, "You will see!"

* * *

The children poured over us. A typical ten year old, Santosh squirmed with embarrassment when I hugged him and kissed his cheek in front of the other boys. Sibani and Pinky squeezed between others as a chair was pulled up for me, to ensure their places pressed right up against my side. Daina held my hand, her face tilted up to me with her sweet smile.

"Hello, how are you?" I asked as I hugged her against me.

"I am fine, thank you," she answered politely. "How are you?"

Although she was a little taller, she was wearing the exact same pink dress she'd had on the last time I saw her. Every few moments she picked up my hand and held it to her lips, covering the backs of my fingers in little kisses. *Smack, smack, smack* against my skin, over and over. Not a day had gone by since the previous March that I hadn't thought of her, and the other kids; but it wasn't until I saw them again, felt their presence all around me, that I realized just how much I had missed them.

The initial commotion of our arrival began to subside and chai and cookies were brought. The children circled around and sang for us. They began with a version of "My Bonnie Lies Over the Ocean," only this one had been modified. Instead they sang, "My Baxter lies over the ocean," and "My Shelley lies over the ocean,"… "Oh, bring back my Caroline to me."

When the singing wound down Papa came to Baxter and then to me, taking our hands and thanking us for coming. He asked if the children remembered us.

"Yes!" they screamed in unison.

Next he took Chandler's hand. "Now, Shelley has brought her daughter, just to meet you," he announced. "She is your sister now."

Chandler smiled bashfully. She seemed embarrassed at the attention, just like the kids often were. Her chair was surrounded by the groupies she'd already drawn – sisters Mami and Sumi, Rahel and Sima. All younger girls who crowded her lap and played with her hair. They pulled it between their fingers and brushed it; braiding it over and over, securing it with elastic fasteners before quickly taking them out to refashion the style. The scene made me think of the hairdo Barbie I had as a child, the big doll's head on a plastic tray that came with clips, combs and curlers for styling. Chandler had quickly become these girls' real-life Barbie head.

Older girls, too, hovered nearby watching. Santa, Barsa and Sunita – adolescents who were much more interested in this girl their own ages than us adults. But they had outgrown the hand-holding and lap-sitting; by their ages it wasn't cool to show such enthusiasm and so they stood nonchalantly by, missing nothing.

* * *

The next morning I sat quietly with Papa in the courtyard under the mango tree, while the children studied.

He was explaining to me the ridicule and slurs that the orphans faced from surrounding villagers. He was driving one of the boys in to the town's school late one day, on his ancient little motor scooter, when they passed a school bus full of kids.

"Do you know, the children leaned out the window and laughed at him," Papa told me. "They yelled, 'Slumdog! Slumdog!'" He leaned forward, his eyes piercing mine in one of his intense stares, as if daring me to contradict him. He waited silently for the meaning of the incident to fully sink in, for me to comprehend the social stigmatization his kids faced every day. Finally he pulled out a handkerchief and lifted his glasses, pressing the linen to his eyes.

I could see how the incident had affected him; when his children hurt, Papa hurt. In a society still heavily influenced by the caste system, these young people remained "untouchables" to everyone outside the cocoon of the ashram.

* * *

The day was hot, the air heavy and still. The only respite from the Indian summer which lasted from mid March until July was to avoid the mid-afternoon sun. Most people rested during those hours, seeking shelter indoors and avoiding activity. Children and adults alike disappeared as everyone in the ashram wandered off for naps. Chandler and I went to an upstairs room to take rest, lying across from each other on small beds covered with hand-embroidered throws.

Mama came in and sat on the edge of Chandler's bed. She stroked Chandler's face and patted her hair. "My sweetie," she said.

It was a nickname that stuck. From that moment Chandler's given name was forgotten by all and she became known simply as "sweetie."

Later, at dinner, Papa came around to give us all seconds, and then thirds. When we told him, "No, Papa, I have plenty," or "I'm full," he merely said, "OK, you take just one!"

As soon as the meal was over and their plates washed, the kids were upon us again. Santosh took my arm. "Dance," he said. "Come, watch dance." Chandler, Baxter and I followed him into his dormitory. A room of about twenty by twenty feet, lined along all the walls were the boys' bunk beds. Foot lockers were stowed under the bottom beds and shirts hung from rows of pegs. Posters of Ganesh and Shiva covered the walls, along with artwork the boys had done. In the open middle of the room, seven or eight boys were dancing like crazy.

Santosh jumped right in, bouncing around with frenetic energy and hamming it up for his audience. He was usually very reserved and quiet, sometimes moody and withdrawn even. I had never seen him so extroverted, taking center stage; and was a little taken aback, though pleased, to witness this new side of him. He jumped around to the drumbeats and mandolins on the radio, glancing over every

few minutes to make sure I was watching him. Chandler
and I laughed and clapped as Baxter encouraged the boys,
pushing their energy to an even more dynamic pace.
Santosh took his outer shirt off and twirled it above his
head, dancing in his white undershirt.

A few girls ventured in to see what all the commotion
was about. Daina and Santa took Chandler's hands and
then mine and dragged us toward their dorm, eager to get
in on the action. The pack of boys followed. A radio was
turned on, and they were off. Teenagers Charu, Sangeeta,
Saraswati and Santa led the pack, while some of the
younger girls like Daina and Sibani joined in. Forming three
chorus-line style rows, they performed complex and
completely synchronized Bollywood dances. They shook
their hips and twirled around, bent down toward the floor
and then jumped up with their hands snaking together
above their heads in time to the Hindi pop music.

Ultra-shy Mami and Sumi clung tightly to Chandler,
occasionally hopping down to mimic the moves from the
sidelines. The second they caught one of us looking they
giggled and ran off to hide. Tiny Papuni stood off to the
side, trying to follow the big girls' movements and dance
steps.

Baxter and his son James were pulled into the room,
and within seconds were jumping around the dance floor
too. This encouraged Santosh, Tapas, Govinda and the other
boys to dance alongside the girls. Soon it was like a mosh
pit in the room, the middle of the floor between the bunks
packed with bodies, laughter and screaming and music

drowning out everything else. All we were missing was a strobe light.

In the middle of all this, I caught sight of Mama walking in at the far end of the room. She stood for a moment watching the disruption we had encouraged, lips pressed together and her brow knotted in consternation. Then, she shook her head and just turned and walked back out without a word. She was the disapproving house mother who would still rather pretend she didn't see anything than break up the party.

* * *

That wasn't the only party we all enjoyed together. Our visit extended over the Indian holiday of Holi, the festival of colors. Originally a celebration of the fertility of the land and good harvests, Holi is commemorated with folk songs and dances, and colored powders or water which everyone throws all over each other. As we left our hotel at nine in the morning, the streets were already filled with music and dancing, and crowds covered with the colored powders. Shops were closed, and many groups carried shrines as they marched with abandon.

At the ashram the boys met us at the entrance path, bouncing around to a pop song blaring from loudspeakers. They were off school for the holiday and full of energy. Some faces were already covered in yellow or purple paint. We were swept into the current of jumping bodies and to the courtyard, where a tent made of colorful saris and decorations had been erected. Babu, Papa's son, greeted us with a bowl of yellow powder.

"Happy Holi!" he exclaimed as he pressed a smudge of yellow on each of our foreheads.

Sibani, Daina, Mami and Sumi drew Chandler away from the dancing boys and to the playground to swing with them. I watched for a moment, Chandler flying high into the air with Mami and Sumi screaming from her lap as Daina and Sibani called, "Didi, look! Didi!" from the slide and monkey bars.

Papa welcomed Baxter and me while the boy pack raced by. I had a glimpse of Tapas, a twelve year old who could only be called beautiful; but today the crown of his head was covered with bandages. Baxter noticed, too.

"Papa, what's wrong with Tapas?" he inquired.

Papa sighed heavily. "Oh, Tapas, he's a very naughty boy. Last night, he tried to sneak out of the ashram."

"For the Holi festivities going on out in the streets?" Baxter asked.

"Hai, yes I think so," Papa said. "He climbed to the top of the wall and then fell off. His head is bleeding. When we ask him what happened, he tells us that he fell in the bathroom." Papa clucked his tongue against the roof of his mouth in dismay at the lie. "He's a very naughty boy," he repeated. Tapas zipped by again, the injury caused by his mischief clearly not slowing him down.

Papa reached up and grabbed the bell rope, clanging the brass bell loudly to start the program. The adults were seated in orange plastic chairs while the children sat on the

ground in front of us, under the tent. A table in the far
corner of the tent held the radio system and a microphone,
as well as a few instruments. A male staff member took up a
drum and another played a small accordion while Papa led
the singing. Between each song he explained its meaning for
the benefit of his guests.

When the singing was over, a group of boys led by
Bikram, Alouk and Rashikanta put on a play. With their
make-up and fake mustaches, I couldn't tell who was who
from my seat. It was funny, even without understanding the
words. It was about an incorrigible schoolboy who refused
to mind the rules; one young actor wore a flesh-colored
plastic "bald" cap on his head, with gray hair puffing out
below it, playing the elder. He entered the stage bent over
and hobbling, over-acting like crazy to play every move for
a laugh.

Next on the program were traditional dance
performances by Santa, Sangeeta, Charu, Meena, Saraswati
and Taru. The girls' costumes, jewelry and face paint were
spectacular and their choreography complex and lovely.
Caroline leaned over to me as we watched.

"They've been taking dance lessons and practicing for
weeks," she said.

As the third routine began, the "elder" from the play
shuffled out with the girls and tried to dance with them,
eliciting gales of laughter and threatening to throw the
dancers off. They didn't falter one bit, and completed their
routine in spite of his antics and the crowd's amusement at
the distraction.

Once the performances were over, Holi was played in earnest. Four neighborhood men came into the courtyard, covered head to toe in deep magenta and holding plastic bags filled with the powder. They headed straight to Caroline, laughing while one wiped a huge streak of purple across her cheek. Coming to each of us in turn, they smeared the dark powder on our cheeks and noses. A younger neighbor gave Chandler a fuchsia mustache.

The children took this marking of us as permission to attack. Handfuls of yellow, green, orange and pink powders were grabbed from bowls set along the courtyard and color flew everywhere, no holds barred. We chased each other down, smearing color on faces and in hair. Baxter caught Sima and covered her cheeks in bright yellow. Papa even got in on the action, slapping Baxter's son, James, on the side of the head with green as James closed his eyes and tried to squirm out of Papa's grasp. Some of the kids produced water guns, shooting colored water at us – a clearly unfair advantage. All the while the speakers blared a favorite song: "Just Chill!" But the kids were nowhere near chilling.

Within fifteen minutes we were all covered, pointing and laughing at each other. I caught a glimpse of Madhu, the house mother who had befriended me the year before. She was completely purple – only her eyes were showing. She tried not to giggle as she chased the kids who had targeted her in mock anger. Even Papa was smeared with yellow and orange. With the powders gone, everyone lined up to be handed small paper bags of sweets and slices of juicy watermelon. The fruit's sweetness exploded in my mouth with a ripeness richer than I had ever tasted in a melon before. It even tasted pink. Soon a hundred yellow and purple and green people sat in the courtyard, slurping watermelon as it dripped between their fingers.

* * *

By the end of the week our evening prayer time was held outside due to the heat; the prayer room had become a stifling oven. On our last night, I closed my eyes to savor the sweet voices drifting up toward the stars overhead, breathing them into my soul. I felt completely at peace, content just sitting there with them, just being. The last song faded into the night sky and a silence descended.

Papa thanked us all, ending with "sweetie" Chandler. One by one each child stood up to say "thank you," before running off. I watched each of them in turn, preparing myself to miss them again. The row of exiting children arrived at Salu, as Mami jumped up from her place in front of Salu.

"Thank you!" Mami giggled and darted off. But Salu didn't stand up. She had fallen asleep, sitting there cross-legged on the rug, during prayer. The girl behind Salu nudged her and with half-closed eyes she pushed herself up, groggily stumbling away.

At the car, taking our leave for the last time, the children were all over us. I worked my way through the crush to Papa and Madhu, to bid them goodbye also. Some of the most reserved kids, those who had been reluctant to demand our attention, for the first time threw their arms around us and kissed our cheeks, told us they loved us. I squeezed Santosh and Daina in tight hugs, reminding them to study hard. I promised them once again that I would be back.

Rahel, one of Chandler's most devoted fans, stood silently in front of her. Offering up a bouquet of flowers tightly in her small fist Rahel's eyes were cast downward, her always impish smile a flat line, too sad to look up at Chandler. Rahel's dejection was too much for my daughter, who started to cry. I hurried to get her and myself to the vehicle before the send-off became too unbearable.

I shuttled Chandler into the car but as soon as I shut the door behind us it opened again. I braced myself for more drawn-out farewells from the kids, but it was Caroline who put her arms around me. As before, she was staying behind to do more work.

"I didn't want you to leave without saying goodbye," she mumbled into my hair. "Thank you so much for coming, for your support, for loving these kids," she said. We hugged tightly and then she closed the door and we were quickly out the gates. Chandler and I sat in the back seat, not looking at each other as she clutched Rahel's flowers.

Throughout the long hours of travel Chandler wept intermittently. "I don't want to go home," she sobbed that night in the hotel. In the security line at the Delhi airport the next day tears slowly leaked from her eyes and trickled down her cheeks. She cried silently on the plane as it lifted

off Indian soil and left it behind, carrying us back home
again.

---

lii The Joint United Nations Programme on HIV/AIDS (UNAIDS),
the United Nations Children's Fund (UNICEF), and the United
States Agency for International Development (USAID),
Children on the Brink 2004: A Joint Report of New Orphan
Estimates and a Framework for Action, July 2004.

liii The Times of India, "Overseas adoptions from India drop to
the lowest," October 14, 2007.

liv India Together, "Adoption Tales" by Swapna Majumdar,
October 23, 2005.

lv Span, "Adoption Option: Growing More Popular" by E. Wayne,
September/October 2005.

"You must not lose faith in humanity. Humanity is an ocean; if a few drops of the ocean are dirty, the ocean does not become dirty."

–Mahatma Gandhi

Being the Change

"Santosh is one of the boys."

I looked at Papa in surprise. Shortly before leaving India, he and Caroline and I sat under the shade of the mango tree while he related to us the difficulties he was having with some of the adolescent boys. A group of them were going off to classes in the morning, but then sneaking back into the ashram shortly thereafter to play or nap. It had been occurring on a fairly regular basis, exasperating both Papa and the staff.

"Santosh?" I questioned. "He's been skipping school?"

"Hai, yes," Papa said. "I don't know what to do. We don't have enough people to watch every child every minute. I tell them they must get their education…" He trailed off, raising his hands in a gesture of defeat.

I glanced at Caroline. Part of me wanted to laugh a little, at the image of this small band of renegade boys pulling a Huckleberry Finn to have a good time. But of course, I did not want to make light of the problem, and was well aware of the importance of an education for all these kids. Their futures had been compromised enough with the odds they already had stacked against them: abandonment or orphanhood, poverty, caste. Without a good education the future grew much bleaker. It was their ticket out.

"Do you think I should talk to Santosh?" I asked both Caroline and Papa.

Papa nodded his head vigorously. "I have talked, and still they are doing this. He will listen to you."

I had halfway hoped Papa would decline my offer. Until then I had been the fun aunt who only had to play games and have a good time and bring treats. But, it was a long-term relationship I had embarked on, not only with Santosh and Daina but with all the children, and Papa as well. I knew that going into it, and now the time had come for the aspect of the adult/guardian role that was not so fun – the arm of discipline. I was going to have to be the bad guy.

Later that day, there was a lull in the activities and I pulled Santosh aside for a quiet moment. His English had improved but was still limited, so I needed to make sure he understood. "How is school?" I began.

"Good."

"Do you study hard?"

"Yes."

"What do you want to be when you grow up?"

Santosh thought about this for a moment. "A dancer," he said. I suppressed a smile at the memory of him dancing in the mosh pit party when we'd first arrived. Like most children, his adult career plans changed with regularity; when I'd first met him, he wanted to be a painter. In one letter to me he'd written that he wanted to be a soldier when he grew up.

I paused, choosing my words carefully. "Papa tells me that sometimes you don't go to school."

Santosh looked down, not meeting my eyes. He seemed embarrassed that I knew this; it had not occurred to him that Papa might tell me.

"Papa said that you and some other boys leave school and miss classes," I continued. "You know that school is very important, don't you?" His nod was an almost imperceptible movement.

"You need to go to school every day, Santosh. You need to study hard and do well in school to be a dancer when you grow up. You need to know your English well so you can be anything you want to be."

He nodded again, but was clearly sulking at the reprimand. The last thing I wanted was for him to feel bad or think I was mad at him, so I put my arm around his shoulders and hugged him to me. "You're a very smart boy, Santosh. Do you know that? You are *very* smart. You can do anything you want to. I'm very proud of you, and it will make me happy if you go to school every day and work hard."

Santosh continued to look at the ground. I patted his back. "You will go to school every day, and not leave classes? You will study hard?" He nodded. "Okay. Do you want to get my camera and take some pictures?" I stood up.

He loved snapping photos with my camera, and I sometimes entrusted it to him as my "official photographer." He smiled and perked up, and I took his hand. "Come on, let's go."

* * *

A few weeks after I returned home, I received a letter sent by The Miracle Foundation. It was written by Santosh in Oriyan and translated by Bubu, one of the house mothers. He talked about the fun of the visit, sent wishes for our good health, and asked Chandler to write him a letter. He also wrote:

"Now I am appearing for my annual exam. We'll get summer vacation next month. I'll let you know my academic result on my next letter. You are right that education is very important for me. Lovingly yours, Santosh."

* * *

The difference that an education, literacy and competency in English makes in the future of a child cannot be overestimated – especially a marginalized or disadvantaged child; a child like Santosh. One of the main factors that makes children vulnerable to street life, trafficking, early marriage, child labor or adult unemployment is lack of education. And, education of its children remains one of India's greatest challenges as a country. Approximately a hundred and thirty-seven million Indian children – nearly half the entire population of the United States – are illiterate. In the six to fourteen year age group, thirty million cannot read at all, forty million recognize only a few letters, and forty million can read some words. Over fifty-five million of these children will not complete four years of school, eventually adding to the illiterate population of India – the largest of any country in the world.[lvi]

At the same time, the higher education system of the country is widely acclaimed, creating a paradox. Nearly sixteen thousand universities and colleges graduate two and a half million students each year; only the U.S. and China produce more college graduates. This production of professionals in India is truly phenomenal, churning out three hundred-fifty thousand engineers every year – twice that of the U.S. In recent years, new law schools are also beginning to produce first-rate attorneys.[lvii] Thomas Friedman, author of *The World is Flat*, wrote in his New York Times column, "They are not racing us to the bottom. They are racing us to the top."[lviii]

Most well-known are the world-class technical institutes. Some of the most prominent corporate CEOs, entrepreneurs, and inventors in the world are graduates of the famed Indian Institutes of Technology, including top executives of US Airways, Citigroup and Sun Microsystems.

Business Week magazine called the IIT graduate "the hottest export India has ever produced." They fill software and tech companies, investment banks and engineering firms all over the globe; an estimated forty percent of start-ups in Silicon Valley are Indian-spawned.[lix]

These students spent their school careers studying in English – a huge advantage over other children in India who never have such a chance. English is recognized as the key to not only the tech centers of Bangalore, but also for jobs in hotels and other service industries. In spite of the quality education available for those with the means, both financially and geographically, to afford it, access to a decent education for families below these top levels is virtually nonexistent. Government schools, particularly in the rural areas, provide a far substandard education for the rest of India's children. A national study found that one out of four teachers in public primary schools was absent each day; of teachers present, half were not teaching. There is also a great disparity between girls and boys – the national male literacy rate is about seventy percent while the female rate is only fifty percent.[lx]

"The government schools are absolutely hopeless," said John Nonhebel, Executive Director of Oasis India, an NGO working with at-risk children and communities. When I visited his office in Mumbai, John told me that lack of education was one of the biggest obstacles to getting out of the poverty trap. "It's a classic scenario that you see repeated time and time again in the slums of the city. The parents were never educated so they don't place a high value on education, and the children repeat that. It's a major issue."

Breaking that cycle could mean huge achievements. Industry in India is booming, and opportunities are there like never before. "But that boom is for the educated," John said. "Without a basic level of literacy, the options are really limited. We need to try to get people to see the value of education and demand it for their child; to encourage people to think of education as a right. Our children deserve to be educated."

John was hopeful that the 2007 national budget, which had set aside large amounts of funding for education, would lead to improvements in the state-run schools. A grass-roots movement is now spreading to reform the schools and demand that English be taught from first grade. Two-thirds of urban children in the three largest states are enrolled in private education, and the poor are also pulling their kids out of government schools at an unprecedented pace, to send them to the private schools that are rapidly spreading in city slums and rural areas across India. Even unrecognized schools in these destitute areas are delivering test scores ten to twenty percent higher than government schools.[lxi]

In addition to private schools, many organizations with tutoring and mentoring based educational programs have sprung up, primarily in the cities. These programs take the education to the children in the streets, the workplaces and the slums where they can be found, providing secondary after-school learning curricula which aim to bridge the gap left by traditional government schooling. For many children, such programs are the only schooling they have.

"Government-run schools are horribly ineffective," said Tina Vajpeyi, Chief Financial Officer of the NGO Akanksha, echoing what John Nohhebel told me. I was introduced to Tina and Akanksha by Deepa Krishnan, the tour guide who showed me around the Dharavi slum in Mumbai. Most of Akanksha's students come from Dharavi and other slum communities in Mumbai.

Akanksha charges that on all dimensions, India is falling far short of delivering quality education to its children. "There is a very high drop-out rate, as much as ninety-eight percent by the tenth standard," said Tina. Of the two percent of students who do make it to tenth standard, many are still illiterate. Even schools that purport to be English standard often teach less privileged children in Hindi instead, shortchanging their futures where they will compete against English speakers for jobs. The average attendance rate at Akanksha, by comparison, is eighty percent and the drop-out rate is less than ten percent.

Tina met me in front of the Nehru Planetarium in the southern end of the sprawling city, where Akanksha runs one of their fifty-five learning centers. The organization began in 1990 with fifteen children and today serves two thousand, six hundred children in program centers like the one at Nehru Planetarium, and another two thousand in school settings. Tina led me inside the cool air-conditioning of the planetarium and down a stairway to the basement rooms where the students meet. She carried herself with the

poise of a model. Her hair was gathered in a loose knot at
the nape of her neck, held back in a utilitarian way meant to
keep it out of the way while she worked, but which lent the
effect of elegance to her smooth face. She reminded me of
Grace Kelly.

As we walked into the room, three groups of children
sat on woven mats on the floor, forming orderly circles
around their teachers and participating in lessons according
to age bracket. These students came to the center for two
and a half hours after their regular school day, every day,
for additional lessons and activities in English and
mathematics. I watched as the group nearest me, four
teenage girls and five boys all wearing navy blue Akanksha
t-shirts that read "Be the Change," analyzed newspaper
articles to improve English skills. "The mastery of English is
the key to open up their future," Tina said.

The space was not large, but was used well and didn't
feel cramped. It was cool and quiet, an environment that
seemed to foster learning. The scuffed and scarred walls
were covered with maps, charts, chalkboards, stories and
assignments completed by the students. The basic idea
behind the initial concept was to employ underutilized
resources. Supplies are donated, volunteers do most of the
teaching, and local doctors provide free medical care and
health camps. Most of the paid staff are part-time teachers
from local communities, often mothers of students. In this
way Akanksha is able to achieve a unique community
partnership, as well as fulfill a secondary goal to empower
women and girls. Female students of the program marry an

average of two to three years later than other girls in the area.

Even so, there is a high turnover of teachers. "It's a stressful job," Tina admitted. Recruiting and retaining committed staff and volunteers remained one of their biggest challenges, along with finding space for the centers and keeping children motivated and committed. If a student could be kept in the program for one to two years the biggest part of the hurdle was crossed. "There is a lot of visible improvement within that time," Tina said. "If you work with them at a young age, you can make a huge change."

Akanksha began with a simple concept by an eighteen year old university student, Shaheen Mistri. She knew there were thousands of slum children who needed and wanted to be educated. There were thousands of college students like herself who had the energy, enthusiasm and time to teach. There existed pockets of available spaces in ideal teaching environments. The idea then, was to bring together the three - kids, student volunteers and spaces - to provide a better education for less privileged children and help keep them in school.

The implementation of the plan was not so simple. Shaheen visited more than twenty schools that rejected her request for space to teach the children. Reactions ranged from claims that her idea was too revolutionary, to fears that "those children" would bring dirt and disease to the other students. Finally the principal of the Holy Name

School, Friar Ivo D'Souza, opened his doors and the first Akanksha center found its home.

Acquiring space was only the first challenge. It proved equally difficult to find those first children and convince them and their parents to come to the learning center. Parents asked Shaheen what a young girl who didn't even speak Hindi could possibly teach their children. But Shaheen persisted, recruiting a group of college student volunteers and persuading the parents to allow their children to try the program. The first fifteen students were brought by bus to the original Akanksha center at Holy Name School.

Shaheen confessed that she didn't really know what she was doing. "There were many days when we had just five children in class, when parents said no, when the children spent more time bathing in the basins than sitting in class," she wrote. "There were days when volunteers asked, 'What difference are we making?' And other days where we just knew that one day it *would* make a difference."

Looking around me in the Nehru center, I could see the progress this small vision with a lot of perseverance and hard work had made. The children here seemed eager to learn. They lingered after class was over, chatting with their teachers or me, in no apparent hurry to leave. I met sixteen-year-old Raju, an artist. He sat down with me on one of the mats, looking out from under thick eyebrows expectantly. I noticed the wispy mustache struggling to grow in above his lip and the eager way he waited to talk to me. His straight, impossibly white teeth were striking when he smiled.

Raju was completing his tenth grade level and had been in Akanksha for six years. I asked what he considered to be the best thing he'd gotten from the program.

"Before Akanksha I thought studies took too much time. I thought I would work instead of going to school," he said. "Now I know that my studies are the most important thing. It leads to a good job. This has changed my life."

Raju had plans to enroll in an art college; his career goal was to be a professional artist. "When did you know you wanted to be an artist?" I asked.

"Since a very young age. I also want to return to Akanksha to be a volunteer art teacher." I asked why he loved painting so much. "The beauty of color inspires me," he answered, smiling modestly. With coaxing, I convinced him to pose for a photo with one of his pieces displayed in the center. He stood next to a self-portrait done with pen and pastel oil sticks and gave me his movie star smile.

I also talked with Ravi, an energetic seventeen year old full of brilliant ideas, with soft eyes and a thin, serious face. Ravi was articulate far beyond his years. He carried himself with the confidence of an adult who knew where he was going in the world. He had just finished his high school final exams and was already training to be a social worker, having completed two years of mentoring and internships at places such as the Make-A-Wish Foundation. He would enter college the next semester and planned to obtain his bachelors of social work and then his master's degree.

"Akanksha was my reincarnation," he proclaimed. "I want to work with families to help them get the services they need. People need help asking for social assistance and reporting problems to government. My biggest hope is to become a good person who has a sensitivity to society." His passion for the work came through in his words. I was impressed by the tremendous knowledge of the field he already possessed, as he launched into an explanation of the Right to Information Act. Ravi would like to work on issues such as HIV/AIDS and the child marriage and dowry system. I had no trouble believing he will accomplish everything he sets his mind to.

"What has been the best thing about being a part of this program?" I asked him, as I had Raju.

"Akanksha has inspired me," said Ravi. "They find out what you're interested in and they help get you on a path for that."

The culture of service that Ravi possessed was one Akanksha seeks to foster in the organization and all its students. Besides education, they provide mentoring and a sense of self-esteem. Many graduates are now trainee teachers or social workers and serve as role models to younger students. The Social Leadership Program focuses on giving children an understanding of social issues and helps them become agents of change in their own communities. Akanksha students have volunteered with tsunami relief efforts, Bombay Hospital pediatric ward and local school renovations. Such projects not only foster the value of service in the children, but give them a level of status and importance to the community – a first for many of them.

"We've been around long enough to prove ourselves to the children, parents and community," Tina said as the students slowly left for the day. "We encourage them to dream a little bigger than they otherwise would."

As I left, too, Tina walked outside with me fifty paces from the Nehru Planetarium and pointed out the slum across a small canal, where the students came from. It was family living on top of family in squalor. Most of them were recent migrants from outlying villages who worked as daily laborers or scrap collectors. Very few possessed voting cards and their children lacked birth certificates in large numbers. The sturdier homes of the slum had tin roofs that were held in place with rocks, while others were covered simply with pieces of plastic. There was no running water. The canal was a stagnant, brackish cesspool filled with trash and sewage.

All of this was within a hundred yards of the pristine Nehru Planetarium where Tina and I stood, and the twenty-story circular office tower that rose up behind us. The modern buildings were surrounded by lush landscaping and acres of emerald green grass being watered by sprinklers which blithely ran in the middle of the hot day. I wondered what the slum residents must think when they looked across the canal, separating them as if by eons, at the precious water being poured so meticulously into the ground.

* * *

When families struggle to feed themselves and even clean water remains painfully scarce, education plays a minimal, too often expendable, role to many of India's poor. Organizations like Akanksha and Pratham, a much larger non-profit educational program, employ a preventative approach to decrease the vulnerability of children living in such poverty to ending up on the streets, trafficked or in child labor. Pratham runs learning centers very similar to Akanksha, but on a larger scale throughout India. Originally parented by UNICEF in 1994, the program began in Mumbai slums such as Dharavi where Pratham reaches about thirty thousand children each year with literacy programs, preschools, computer classes and teacher training. It quickly expanded to Delhi and other cities, launching a nationwide program called Read India in 2002 with a mission of "every child in school and learning well."

An incident in a Delhi slum called Zakhira demonstrates the difficulty that children living in these areas often face just getting to school. Zakhira is an illegal shantytown balanced precariously – and dangerously – in a triangle formed between three train tracks. Trash and defecation clog the tracks where trains speed by mere feet from corroding tin and plastic homes. Not long ago a young child was run over and killed by a train as he followed his mother to school. When the police came, the grieving mother had to deny the child was hers to avoid prosecution for endangering the lives of passengers on the train.[lxii]

Other students must cross these very same tracks to attend the nearest school, a risk that most parents don't allow. The largely migrant families that make up Zakhira rarely stay for more than a few months. These challenges, coupled with the great poverty, make many parents reluctant to send their children for an education. When Pratham set up their program in this area in 2005, many members of the organization saw the Zakhira venture as one of its most difficult and wondered if the possibility to teach anything substantial there even existed. Slow improvements have come, however. Children who previously knew nothing of India's Independence Day now celebrate in Zakhira's own commemoration festival. The community was soon swarming with children able to count and read the Hindi alphabet; seemingly small accomplishments, but something few in the area could do before.[lxiii]

Because Pratham works in many small villages as well as cities, its staff see first-hand the educational gap between rural and urban India. Program Director and co-founder Farida Lambay, speaking to me by telephone from her Mumbai office, stressed the necessity of attacking the problem of illiteracy in the poor rural areas and underdeveloped states. The large Indian cities are full of migratory workers who come looking for better jobs and an escape from the failing education and health systems of the villages. These rural migrants end up populating the urban slums in large numbers, increasing the burden on faltering educational systems in the cities. Pratham believes that attacking the problem at the rural level, where children sorely lack any educational opportunities and where many of the urban poor come from, is the key to literacy for every child.

"We mapped out where the kids in Mumbai were coming from, which rural districts, and we began working there," Ms. Lambay explained. The first such rural model was implemented in Bihar, largely considered one of India's most backward states with the lowest literacy levels, and today approximately six out of ten Pratham learning centers are now in these rural areas. Across the country, Pratham has supported a million children in twenty-one states since its inception, and has attained literacy with over a hundred-sixty thousand. With a scope, size and vision that hasn't been attained by another NGO or even the government, Pratham has managed to accomplish results where many others have failed. In 2000 the World Bank named Pratham one of the top three "most innovative development projects."[lxiv]

"Every child has a fundamental right to a family and an education," Ms. Lambay stressed. "You can't leave out children who are at the bottom of the ladder."

---

lvi Pratham, www.pratham.org

lvii BBC News, "India's Faltering Education System" by Kaushik Basu, August 18, 2006.

lviii The New York Times, "A Race to the Top" by Thomas Friedman, June 3, 2005.

lix BusinessWeek, "India's Whiz Kids" by Manjeet Kripalani, December 7, 1998.

lx Asha for Education, http://www.ashanet.org/projects/state-view.php?s=28.

lxi Newsweek, "India's Education Boom," by Gurcharan Das, February 28, 2006.

lxii Pratham, Hope Amidst Despair by Chetan Narain, page 22. 2006.

lxiii Pratham, Hope Amidst Despair by Chetan Narain, page 23. 2006.

lxiv Pratham website,
   http://www.pratham.org/aboutus/aboutus.php

"If you can't feed a hundred people, then feed just one."

–*Mother Teresa*

Lost and Found

Dr. Manjeet Pardesi listened in horror as the young woman related her story. Neela had recently come to the home in Rourkela because she had heard it was a place where unwed mothers and their babies would be taken care of without abuse or judgment. The twenty-three year old was pregnant with her landlord's baby and didn't know what to do. There was no one to help her.

Neela had been caring for her eight year old brother and ten year old sister in their remote village in Jharkhand state, just north of Orissa, since their parents died several years earlier. Dire financial circumstances caused the small family to owe money to the landlord, who intimidated and coerced the girl into a physical relationship while the young siblings were sent into bonded labor to pay off the debt. An outreach worker brought Neela to the Miracle Foundation home for delivery.

"The physical intimacy was not done due to love but due to fear," Manjeet wrote me in an email. "In other words, you can term this as rape."

While this seemed obvious, it was a brave and somewhat controversial statement for Manjeet to make. Such physical and sexual violence against Dalits, once considered the "untouchables," is widespread and rarely considered abuse or even a crime at all. In an extensive investigation of caste-based discrimination conducted in 2006, Human Rights Watch found that rape of Dalit women by landlords like what Neela endured is all too common. Dalit victims of rape face significant obstacles when attempting to report the crime to police or to bring a case before the courts. Perpetrators are rarely charged or punished, and their victims are usually the ones ostracized from the community – so much so that rape survivors are often considered unmarriageable.[lxv]

"Caste is very much the root of the problem," said Manjeet. "The government gives them certain privileges, but due to acute poverty and caste dogma these things happen. The people who are Dalits are at the receiving end of exploitation."

He began bombarding Neela's landlord with constant communication on behalf of her brother and sister. "Initially he was reluctant to part with the children," reported Manjeet, "until he was informed that the matter would be turned over to the police."

At that point the landlord finally agreed to return the children from bonded servitude in exchange for the money owed him. Miracle Foundation staff drove to Calcutta, where the children had been put into labor, to bring them to live with their elder sister at the home in Rourkela. Manjeet paid the price of their debt: Twenty-five U.S. dollars.

Neela's young brother and sister were freed from their life of bondage, but for most such children freedom never comes. Child trafficking, indentured servitude, factory labor and the sex trade comprise an "industry" that huge numbers of children fall victim to, disappearing into an underground world. The conditions these children are forced into essentially amount to nothing more than slavery, two hundred years after legislation was passed which made the practice illegal. And this is slavery at its ugliest, most evil core, slavery of the most vulnerable among us: children.

Child laborers and prostitutes exist in such large numbers for a simple, yet horrific, reason: they are cheap commodities. Children cost less than cattle; while a cow or buffalo costs an average twenty thousand rupees, a child can be bought and traded like an animal for five hundred to two thousand rupees.[lxvi] They can be paid the least, exploited the most, and due to their youth and vulnerability have virtually no power against their oppressors.

While factories that exploit children in China and Central America are often in the news, India is the country most plagued by this human rights abuse, having the highest number of child laborers in the world. Official estimates of the number of these children vary greatly, often by definition of who such children are. The UNICEF

website reports 12.6 million children engaged in hazardous occupations, but this figure is according to the 2001 government census; because more than half of all children born in India are never registered and records are not kept or reported on child workers, it may safely be assumed that this estimate is extremely low.[lxvii] The official Indian government figure, based on a Labour of Ministry survey that is more than twenty years old, is forty-four million.

At the other end of the spectrum Human Rights Watch estimates between sixty and a hundred fifteen million[lxviii], and Global March Against Child Labor contends that as many as one hundred million children are believed to be working, "many under conditions akin to slavery," with an estimated fifteen million in bonded servitude.[lxix] Bonded labor or servitude is defined as work in which children are indentured to the employer in order to pay off a debt. Few sources of traditional credit or bank loans exist for those living in poverty. The earnings of the bonded children are less than the interest on these informal loans, ensuring that they will typically never be able to pay off the debt. Thus, they become in effect a slave of the "employer."[lxx]

The Human Rights Watch conducted extensive investigations into child labor in India in both 1996 and 2003, both times finding widespread abuses among millions of children and very little legal or practical protection being offered. In the silk industry, for example, HRW investigator and counsel Zama Coursen-Neff discovered bonded children as young as seven working in factories in three different states. She interviewed a girl called Nallanayaki.

Since the age of nine, Nallanayaki had been laboring thirteen hours a day in a silk factory to pay off a $146 loan her parents took from her employer. Her salary of less than seventeen cents per day, however, meant that her freedom would never be earned during her lifetime – passing on the debt to her own children and continuing the cycle.

The investigation also concluded that caste-based discrimination is at the heart of bonded labor and hugely intertwined with child exploitation. Nallanayaki, like the vast majority of such laborers, is a Dalit. The caste system sustains the mechanisms by which bonded labor thrives, through the centuries-old expectations of free or vastly underpaid work, discrimination and violence against Dalits, and the extreme marginalization that prevents them from accessing resources available to other members of society.[lxxi]

Coursen-Neff reported that these children were forced to dip their hands into boiling water to make the silk thread, handle dead silkworms, breathe fumes that made them ill and worked in cramped, damp rooms. They did not attend school and were often beaten by their employers or burned with hot tongs if they fell asleep.[lxxii]

When I read this, I had to close the report and set it aside. I felt sick to my stomach. It seemed more than I could bear to think about; but at the same time, I couldn't bear not to. My mind reeled at how people could do this to other people – especially defenseless children. The work of another journalist, Philip Gourevitch, popped into my mind. In his brilliant book, *We Wish to Inform You That Tomorrow We Will be Killed With Our Families* about the 1994

Rwanda genocide, Gourevitch wrote of his fascination with the peculiar necessity of imagining what is, in fact, real. The way a thing, even as it was happening that very moment in the world around us, could be so horrific that we could still only imagine it, our minds refusing to accept it as reality.

I understood exactly what he meant. In a way, it was far easier to let the vastness of these atrocities slip past my mind which didn't want to accept them as possible, which became too easily overwhelmed and despairing at the thoughts. But, I knew to do that would be, for me, an unforgivable act. I *did* know. Now I could only decide if I chose instead to look away. And if I did that, if everyone did that, who would be left stand up for these children?

Gourevitch similarly examined his own pain and difficulty at spending so much time steeped in the genocide. "The best reason I have come up with for looking closely into Rwanda's stories," he concluded, "is that ignoring them makes me even more uncomfortable about existence and my place in it."[lxxiii]

* * *

In Calcutta, only miles from where Neela's siblings were bought out of bonded labor, a man named Swapan Mukherjee has dedicated nearly two decades of his life to rescuing such children. Swapan led the formation of the non-profit Centre for Communication and Development (CCD) to assist destitute children in 1978, just after receiving his Master's of Social Work degree. In its early years CCD focused primarily on education.

Then in 1995, an explosion at Nawab Fireworks factory just outside Calcutta killed twenty-three children who were working there illegally. The factory employed only children – fifteen hundred of them, working from six am to six pm for an average weekly wage of sixty-five rupees, about $1.50. The explosion rocked the entire surrounding area. Trees were uprooted and concrete pillars along with children's bodies were tossed in the air and landed in a nearby pond. The factory owners were not fined for employing illegal child labor nor otherwise charged for the deaths or unsafe working conditions. Swapan was outraged.

"The factory refused all responsibility for the tragedy," he told me, disbelief still ringing in his voice twelve years after the incident. I went to Calcutta to visit his organization a week after leaving Mumbai in 2007, as I traveled the country researching the issues endangering children. Ultimately, Swapan himself had taken the factory owners to court and won a judgment for compensation to all the victims' families. "From there we moved to a focus on child protection and safety," he said.

Since that time CCD has rescued almost two thousand children from a horrific array of abusive situations, including mutilation by begging rings to make them more effective at soliciting. In 2001, the Muktaneer Home for Destitute Children was opened in Calcutta for children who did not have a home to return to, or whose families were too poor to care for them – children like Sahiful.

Sahiful was put into indentured labor at the age of four, after his father died of tuberculosis. With their mother suffering from mental illness it fell to this small boy and his siblings to somehow put food into their mouths. Sahiful's first job was agricultural work, crushing hard earth with a brick. The demanding work earned him the equivalent of twenty cents per day. Due to the seasonal nature of the job, in the off season he was put to work tending goats from sunrise to sunset. For this he earned two portions of rice per day. When he once lost a goat under his watch, his employer beat him and denied him food for three days.

Today thirteen year old Sahiful's life is very different. Rescued at the age of six and brought to Muktaneer, which means "Open Sky" in Hindi, his life was freed from exploitation. There he began receiving four good meals a day, was given his own bed and was allowed to play for the first time in his life. He began attending school and his family was also provided assistance.

When I arrived at Muktaneer, the gates swung open to reveal forty boys rushing out to greet my taxi. I immediately picked Sahiful out of the crowd from his photo in the newspaper article I'd first read about CCD. He was very tall for his age, standing a full head above the others, an attractive bright-eyed boy full of boundless, optimistic energy. His easy grin revealed a chipped front tooth and his light hazel eyes sparkled in the night lights shining over the building's entrance.

Sahiful is special not only because of his easy charm and quick intelligence. He also just happens to be an international award-winning filmmaker.

As Swapan recovered Sahiful and other children, he photographed and videotaped the investigations – the children's conditions, their lives and their rescues – to use as documentation for prosecution. Sahiful was fascinated with the camera. "He and the other boys wanted to document their own lives, tell their own stories," said Swapan. "They revealed a rare keenness to engage in story writing, photography and film direction."

And so they began filming themselves, led by the camera work of Sahiful. The boys wrote, directed and produced their own scenes, drawing on their experiences as well as their hopes and dreams. The result was a beautiful short film called *I Am*, a twenty-minute documentary that explored questions of the seemingly impossible. The film began with one of the child actors asking, "Do you want to know who I am?" The children went on to ask such questions of wonder as, "If fish sleep with their eyes open, why can't we?" and "Why do stars disappear when the sun rises?" They were questions that these boys never had the luxury of asking before, in their small hard lives where the only questions were those of where their next meal was coming from and how to avoid pain.

I Am won Grand Prize at the 2004 International Children's Film Festival in Athens, and came to the attention of the Australian press where it ran as a major story in The Age newspaper, the article I read about these

incredible young people. It was even featured on the Oprah
Winfrey show.

After the boisterous group introduction to Muktaneer,
Swapan led me down the main hallway of the home to his
cramped and cluttered office. I was served chai and biscuits
as Swapan settled down in front of his computer. His gray
trousers and neat, though worn, white pin-striped oxford
shirt hung loosely on his thin frame. Thick hair was combed
elegantly back from his high forehead, peppered slightly
with silver; but his trimmed beard was solid black. He
pushed his glasses up the bridge of his nose in distraction as
he moved stacks of papers from in front of the monitor to
show me the boys' newest film, *The Inner Eye*. A moving
story of an HIV-positive villager ostracized from his
community, its message is AIDS awareness as shown
through a blind man who bestows compassion and help on
the banished neighbor through the "inner eye" of his heart.

As we watched I heard scurrying footsteps outside the
curtained doorway, and then saw eyes peeking around the
sides of the curtain as the boys spied on me viewing their
film. When I noticed them, they giggled and dropped the
curtain back into place; their feet beneath it, however,
continued to give their presence away.

When the movie was over, Swapan and I moved to a
classroom next door with Sahiful and a few of the other
boys who had written or directed films. They sat at wooden
desks and looked at me expectantly, polite and orderly. I
handed my camera to a boy of about ten to be the official
photographer. He ran in and out of the room as I talked to

the group, taking pictures of both us and children eating or studying in other parts of the home.

I turned to Sahiful, who seemed to always have a smile on his face. "How is your life different now?" I asked, and Swapan translated into Bengali.

"Before I lived here, I didn't study, I didn't go to school," Sahiful said. "I could not even dare to dream I would ever sleep on a cot with a mattress. When I came here, I can go to school. I learned about photo and film. I love it!" As he spoke I looked at his clear, innocent face filled with enthusiasm, and tried to imagine him as a small boy laboring in the fields for ten to fourteen hours a day. It was almost impossible to do.

In the brochure for *The Inner Eye* Sahiful is described as "a creative, kind and generous young man who has become a leader at Muktaneer." After spending only a short while with the boy his natural leadership skills were evident. He had a clear passion for the art of filmmaking, and it wasn't about being the star or personal accolades. When I asked him what he liked most about all the praise that *I Am* and the other films have received, he said he enjoyed the attention and the fact that people talked to him. They treated him like somebody important – likely for the first time in his life. But what was his greatest reward?

"When we got first prize, all the boys here were very happy," he replied, a huge grin on his face. It was definitely a team effort here, and the praise was for them all.

The child slave turned filmmaker has filmed or directed two other movies since *I Am*, both of which also received awards, and they have won him travel to Athens, Cyprus and Melbourne; places he had not even heard of a short time ago. The filmmaking and travel for awards are all dependent on donations raised by CCD – a constant struggle, but one that Swapan is completely dedicated to.

"The international film festival has given them a rare chance to see the world in a different light," said Swapan. "Childhood wonders are taking them to a new world of possibilities and recognition."

Sahiful's background is a common story at Muktaneer, where most of the boys came from slave labor conditions or had been kidnapped and sold. Ashikul, also thirteen, sat in the back of the room. Not nearly as quick to smile as Sahiful, Ashikul's early childhood was also one of exploitation and hard labor at a heartbreakingly young age.

Orphaned at four years old, his grandmother first took him in and then his elder brother. Barely eking out survivals of their own, the burden of an additional mouth to feed proved too much for both, who abandoned him. With no one else to turn to Ashikul, five years old by this time, lived on the street where he begged from passersby or did odd jobs at tea stalls and sweet shops in return for food and shelter. Soon he was working in a leather manufacturing business that employed cheap child labor in open defiance of child rights and labor laws.

It was in this illegal factory that CCD found Ashikul in 2000, when he was only six years old. Forty-two percent of the world's leather footwear, often made by small hands like Ashikul's, originates in Asia and the Middle East (principally China, India, Thailand, Indonesia, Pakistan, Iran, and Turkey). A 1995 study by a Delhi research institute found that children under fifteen made up thirty to forty percent of workers in leather manufacturing shops. Such factory work is not only outrageously abusive for a child that age, it is also unhealthy and dangerous. Toxic fumes, chemicals, and hazardous tools and machines are daily risks. The U.S. Department of Labor reported one case where a child fell asleep while cleaning a chemical drum used for tanning, and was killed when the drum was refilled with chemicals as he slept.[lxxiv]

For Ashikul, who had never had anyone offer him food, shelter or kindness without a heavy price, life at Muktaneer was an entirely new experience. Here he was not only cared for and educated, but for the first time he was encouraged to dream. Those dreams turned into films such as *I Am* and its follow-up, *We Are*.

"What are your dreams?" Swapan asked the other boys.

Rinku, fourteen, aspires to become a doctor. "I love science!" he said with enthusiasm. A small and intense boy with sharp eyes and a scar just under his right eyebrow, Rinku's interest in medicine led him to write the newest film I had just watched, *The Inner Eye*. "My inspiration was roadside posters I saw about HIV," he said. "There are many people who do the wrong things. Through my writing and films I hope to inspire others to do the right thing."

"It was my dream to make a movie," Sahiful answered. "Swapan gave me a camera, and I took one photo, and from there I learned all about filmmaking. I can now dream that I can make more and more films, hopefully for the larger screen after some years." He was determined and very passionate about his newfound talents, and I had absolutely no doubt that one day I might hear his name called at the Academy Awards or Cannes Film Festival.

These extraordinary boys have all come a long way from their early childhoods.

* * *

Swapan's work moved across states and international borders as his awareness of the scope of child trafficking grew. In 1996 he was in Delhi when he saw four street children huddled together in tears. "I wanted to know what had happened to them," he said. After some gentle questioning the children were able to identify the men who had trafficked them to the city from their home village.

Swapan reported the traffickers to the police and then traveled to the children's village, Murshidabad, to find their parents. The children were returned home, but Swapan was not satisfied with leaving it at that. He organized a four-member team and spent six months in the village, doing a door to door household survey to find out about other missing children. The responses were dismaying – family after family made reports of kidnapped or runaway children, or those who were promised a good job in the city.

"In those six months we surveyed fourteen hundred

households, and from that effort 364 children who had been trafficked were brought back," Swapan said. CCD began supporting remote villages like Murshidabad with primary schools for children who previously had no educational opportunities – the circumstances in which children are most vulnerable to being exploited and trafficked. Today, there are sixty-five such CCD village schools with nearly ten thousand students attending each year. The organization also advocates with women's and children's rights groups in several states.

Although the Muktaneer Home in Calcutta is only for boys, CCD works with other organizations who provide similar residential and rehabilitation homes for girls. Swapan hopes to one day build a CCD home just for girls; he even has the land, but lack of funding prevents construction from beginning. Like many people doing such work, he told me that he refused to accept government grants because of the corruption and kickbacks involved. Girls as young as seven years old are trafficked across international borders to work in the sex trade – both out of India and into the country from Nepal, Bangladesh and other surrounding nations. Female victims are also forced into India's own thriving sex trade.

Boys from remote districts of West Bengal, the state where Calcutta is located, are also trafficked across international borders, often to Middle Eastern countries for begging during the Muslim pilgrimage of Holy Hajj or to be used as camel jockeys. "They are tied to the necks of the camels, their screaming used to spur on the animals,"

Swapan explained the violent practice. This often results in the child's death.

Every year hundreds of children are flown to Saudi Arabia with fake passports and fictitious parents, who are actually their traffickers. In 1996 Swapan put together a team to conduct a survey in three districts of West Bengal. The survey revealed that over fifteen hundred children had been trafficked to Saudi Arabia between 1992 and 1996. CCD activists helped the parents lodge complaints with the police while Swapan sought immediate intervention from the government.

"But the authorities maintained silence," he said. He and the victim's parents responded with a nonviolent hunger strike in protest against government inaction, which he called "Fast unto Death." As Swapan continued investigating child traffickers, he contacted Amnesty International, Equality Now, and other human rights organizations for assistance. Eventually, CCD was successful in returning home more than four hundred boys from the Middle East, and has been integral in bringing fifty-four child traffickers before the courts. "After this time the government slowly began taking some action," he told me.

* * *

Government action, intervention and enforcement are much too slow, most child labor activists contend. One out of four children reported missing in India are never found. The strong link between missing persons and slavery indicates an immediate need to find and rescue children who have been reported missing. People trafficking is the fastest growing illegal trade in the world, second only to arms. With an estimated revenue of forty-two billion dollars, it is so lucrative that many drug dealers are changing their cargo to human beings. India represents forty percent of the world's human trafficking.[lxxv] In 2007 the South Asia Centre for Missing and Exploited Persons was formed precisely for this reason. "Tracing missing children and women across South Asia before they are exploited is emerging as a key focus area in the efforts to prevent human slavery," wrote Ashley Varghese, Legal Counsel for the organization, in a letter to me.

In direct contradiction to the actual reality, bondage and child labor in industries deemed hazardous have been illegal in India for many decades. The 1976 Bonded Labour System Act was passed with the goal of ending the practice of indentured servitude. The Act "frees all bonded laborers, cancels any outstanding debts against them, prohibits the creation of new bondage agreements, and orders the economic rehabilitation of freed bonded laborers by the state."[lxxvi] Such protection continues to be largely on paper only, having little actual effect because the laws are rarely enforced and its violators seldom prosecuted.

The first child labor law was enacted in February 1933. Since then there have been nine different Indian legislations relating to child labor. The 1986 Child Labor Act states that no child under the age of fourteen shall be put to work in any factory, mine, or hazardous employment, outlined as thirteen occupations and fifty-one processes such as carpet weaving, cigarette making, fireworks and the silk trade. On October 10, 2006 a new law expanded the industries banned for child labor to include domestic service, hotel work and restaurant and tea stall employment.[lxxvii]

But the issue of child labor is not as straightforward as it might appear: child labor is bad, so eliminate it, period. Working children are often seen as a necessity for survival, and as such can be an accepted socio-economic reality in India. Often families themselves place children in such conditions when they feel they have no other choice. Many unsophisticated parents fall prey to promises by recruiters that their children will do light work, go to school, be exposed to more opportunities in the city, and send money back home. They're even told the child will have better marriage possibilities.[lxxviii] Living in poor rural villages without many prospects, these families believe the child will have a better future.

Fueled by controversy over the true causes of the problem, some have strong doubts that simply removing all children from the workplace will solve the child labor problem. Rita Panicker, Director of the Butterflies NGO for street and working children in Delhi, said, "The ban has come without any prior planning for restoration and rehabilitation of children who will be affected. It is ridiculous to think that announcing a ban alone will end child abuse and exploitation."[lxxix]

Butterflies is a strong advocate against child labor, but they operate from an approach of empowering children currently in the labor system at the same time. Butterflies has set up child unions to protect young workers from exploitation and abuse, a youth-run newspaper that provides a voice for these workers, and even a children's development bank. Their empowerment model seeks to equip children with knowledge about their own rights and to give them the means to protect those rights for themselves. Their website states, "Butterflies believes that no child should be working and out of school, but recognizes the reality as being otherwise."

The Human Rights Law Network reported that although child workers are regularly rescued and "paraded before the media," ninety percent or more of them come back to work – often to worse conditions or to end up being sold or trafficked.[lxxx] And in a BBC News report Gerry Pinto, a child rights and protection specialist, said of the 2006 ban: "It will push thousands of children out of the middle-class homes and food stalls, where they have been earning a living and have some sort of shelter, out onto the streets or into prostitution."[lxxxi]

But just how safe these domestic, hotel and restaurant jobs really are is debatable. UNICEF declares that among child laborers, domestic workers are the most invisible.[lxxxii] The reality is that most of these children are virtually enslaved, abused, and send very little if any money home. A recent study by Save The Children found that most child domestic workers labor up to fifteen hours a day with little break for less than twelve U.S. dollars per month. Fully half of them are given no leave time and thirty-seven percent never see their families.[lxxxiii] An extensive research study in the Kolkata area found that sixty-eight percent of child domestic workers had suffered physical abuse and nearly nine out of ten had been victims of sexual abuse.[lxxxiv]

In 2001, an eleven year old domestic worker burst from her master's home, her little body ablaze, after he set her on fire. A neighbor put the fire out with palm mats and the girl was taken to the hospital, where she later died. Elsewhere, a royal couple brought an eight year old orphan boy into their palace compound to work. He was later rescued. The boy suffered from malnutrition and extreme injuries resulting from physical torture, including fractures and severe burns. He reported to authorities that he slept with the household dogs and was once thrown from the palace roof.[lxxxv]

A highly publicized 2006 case received tremendous attention when a ten-year-old domestic worker in Mumbai was murdered by her affluent employers. The girl, Sonu, was reported as a suicide to police, who arrived at the suburban home to find her body hanging from the ceiling fan. An investigation, however, revealed that Sonu had been beaten and then left to bleed to death by her mistress. Her crime? The employer's daughter had caught her trying on lipstick from a dressing table. When the truth came out it caused an uproar in the media.[lxxxvi] Sonu became a sort of poster child against domestic child labor and possibly spurred on the legislation in October of that year which added such work to the list of banned industries for children.

"Domestic work is a very hidden phenomenon," Farida Lambay of Pratham told me. "It's not very easy to go into someone's house and say 'you must stop this.' So, you have to change the mindset of the society. In India we must come to a place where child labor is not acceptable."

Pratham, which aims to give every child an education by taking schools into the slums and workplaces, has been at the forefront of the fight against child labor. Ms. Lambay acknowledged that sometimes children have little choice but to work due to economic reasons. In those cases, when employment is stopped, then rehabilitation and a safety net must be provided to ensure that families and children have the ability to sustain themselves.

She contended that the financial necessity of child labor as a whole is vastly overstated. "When these children work, the economic situation of most families does not improve at all. We must look at why children are really working." She outlined the major factors Pratham identified as perpetuating child labor: Lack of opportunity, lack of education, lack of role models and lack of family or other parental support.

"The unemployment in this country is high," Ms. Lambay continued. "So why are we employing children? Why aren't their parents in these jobs instead?" She paused, and then answered her own question. "Because the children, they can be hired and exploited much more cheaply."

The Global March Against Child Labor, a coalition of two thousand social service organizations in a hundred and forty countries, arrived at the same conclusion about economic necessity. Like Pratham, their findings indicated that children's earnings contribute so little to family income as to be almost meaningless. When children replace adults in the job market, wages are depressed and economic growth is hindered. While millions of children in India work, seventy million adults remain unemployed. Global March's recent studies question poverty as the major cause of child labor, citing the fact that other countries with similar levels of poverty have very different rates of child labor.[lxxxvii]

Pratham found itself in a unique position to view the inside machinations of child labor as they began setting up learning centers in slum areas, taking school to the most at-risk children. Staff members discovered that many of those missing out on their education were working instead. They discovered children six to fourteen years old in sweatshops, sometimes up to eighteen hours a day, and began talking to the owners of these workplaces about setting up Pratham centers within the factories. Although many were reluctant, some owners allowed the children to go to morning school for half an hour to two hours, and then work in the afternoon. Other students learn through India's National Institute of Open Schooling, an initiative in which children can be taught the curriculum at home or through informal education and then appear for their class exams. If they pass the exams, they are given certificates similar to the General Equivalency Degree (GED) in the United States.

Running these learning centers in the workplaces enabled Pratham staff to monitor the situation and conditions of working children. After a while there came a turning point, said Ms. Lambay. "As an organization, we were very uncomfortable with the fact that these children were coming to school and were still working. We realized that education was not enough. We must take a stand against child labor."

This stand turned into a loud and visible campaign after a child died in a Mumbai factory. Pratham began educating business owners about the illegality and harmful effects of employing children. They took their crusade to the highest levels of government, recommending awareness campaigns, involvement of the parents of working children, raids on factories, and more rehabilitation homes for rescued children. Their goal was to have Mumbai declared a child labor free city. "If Mumbai says no to child labor, and Delhi, and Calcutta…soon families will stop sending their kids there to work; children will no longer be trafficked to city factories," said Ms. Lambay

"But the owners were very threatened," she continued. "We were no longer talking about education, but the empowerment of children." Pratham continued the work, along with other organizations such as Save The Children and Stop The Traffik. They initiated police raids, conducted Child Labor Workshops and ultimately rescued twenty-three thousand children from exploitative working conditions. "We must have government and police enforcement against child labor to eradicate it. The owners won't stop on their own. There's no benefits to them," said Ms. Lambay, echoing a familiar weariness with the lack of enforcement and prosecution by authorities.

The Butterflies program has been criticized for supporting the development of working children's unions, a move seen as contrary to the movement against child labor. Although the unions also seek to mobilize public opinion to address the conditions that force children to work, organizations such as Pratham and Global March see such initiatives as contradictory, a direct violation of the stance on eliminating child labor. "Circumstantial compulsion to work due to economic necessity or other reasons do not create a new 'right' of children to work," states the Global March blog. "Forcing young children to work for their own survival is society's repudiation of their fundamental rights."

Butterflies, however, operates from a very different base of reality – until there exists *no* working child, children still in the workplace must be protected. Butterflies wishes to prevent exactly the type of abuses that Sonu endured.

It is a controversy of the child labor movement that is not easily solved. As I talked to people and researched the issues, I found myself having mixed emotions about the different approaches. On the one hand, I completely agree with Pratham and Global March, in their stance that any form of child labor is unacceptable. We should address the reasons children work, support them with a safety net while removing them from such circumstances, protect children from trafficking and abuse, and work globally to ensure an end to all child labor and trafficking.

On the other hand, I understand the reality that Butterflies works within, which is concurrently providing empowerment and protection for those children who *are* in the workplace while working toward the goal of removing them from labor. It doesn't seem that this would legitimize the exploitation of children any more than providing condoms to protect sex workers from AIDS would legitimize their exploitation.

Mostly, it became clear to me that creating a world in which children are free from labor, trafficking and exploitation can only be accomplished from the top down. Only with the full and visible participation of those in power – governments and the corporate world – can the rights of the powerless be upheld. "In a way, rescuing the children is the easy part," Farida Lambay said. "But then – what do you do with them? To really put an end to it, you need to rehabilitate the children, give them an education, support them for the long term; to mainstream them into society."

There have been some encouraging strides. A prominent media campaign called "From WORK to SCHOOL" features several Bollywood stars as well as government officials from the Ministry of Labour and Employment. Another program called Bal Mitra Gram is taking the fight to rural areas, encouraging Indian villages to abolish child labor by agreeing as a community that no child will be put to work. The problem is also being porate level. One of the biggest industries ⸺n in South Asia is rug making. A new program called Rugmark, started by Global March founder Kailash Satyarthi, provides a certification process that labels rugs as manufactured without any form of child labor. Satyarthi plans to extend the labeling program to other products commonly made by children.

The IKEA Group home furnishings company provides another example of how corporations can do business in a socially responsible manner and create awareness for consumers about how their products are manufactured. In partnership with UNICEF, IKEA requires all its suppliers to recognize the Convention on the Rights of the Child and makes regular spot-checks to ensure that no children are working. The UNICEF-IKEA project also helps set up women's self-help groups in the communities in which they operate, and works to ensure that every child is immunized and in school. As UNICEF stated, the project "is founded on the belief that child labour cannot be eliminated by simply removing a child from work...as the child would simply move on to a different employer."[lxxxviii]

The end consumer can make a great impact as well – individuals like you and I, going about our day to day lives. There are many things the average person can do to help end these "industries." The very first step is awareness – choosing to acknowledge it instead of turning away. In the words of Albert Schweitzer, "Think occasionally of the suffering of which you spare yourself the sight."

We can also be conscious of where the goods we buy are coming from. Is it really worth getting something a few dollars cheaper if it is made by slave labor or children? Resources such as "The Better World Shopping Guide" (betterworldshopper.com) provide ethical consumer's guides to avoiding products that are manufactured by employing child labor. They rate the best and worst companies on the planet based on a comprehensive analysis of their social and environmental responsibility over the past twenty years.

We can take action by signing petitions and supporting organizations, such as Global March Against Child Labor, that are working worldwide to end child labor. We can also be politically active, writing our elected officials about our views. Urge them to support the United Nations' Convention on the Rights of the Child – ratified by all countries except Somalia and the United States. Support other international coalitions aimed at ending child labor, trafficking and slavery.

An extraordinary teenager named Om Prakash Gurjar is an inspiring example of the change one individual can affect. Taken from his parents at the age of five to repay his grandfather's debt by performing field and agricultural work, Om Prakash was rescued by activists three years later and taken to live at a rehabilitation center for working children. In school the boy quickly rose to first of his class and got involved in cricket and theater arts. But more remarkable was the activism he undertook to save other children from the fate that was once his own.

When the poor students at his school were asked to pay fees in spite of the fact that government education was supposed to be free, Om Prakash spoke out. He approached the local magistrate and a petition was filed in court decreeing that all monies taken by the school be returned to the parents. The Rajasthan State Human Rights Commission took up the action and created a legal precedent which made education in the entire state accessible to all children.

He also campaigned for birth registration, the first and most basic right of a child which ensures an education and health care, and helps protect him or her from exploitation. Om Prakash visited schools and villages to campaign about the importance of official birth certificates and was personally responsible for the registration of more than five hundred birth documents. Back in his home village, he single-handedly implemented the Bal Mitra Gram program to make the village child labor free.

Perhaps the most striking example of his tireless dedication occurred when he was thirteen. The 2005 World Congress on Child Labour and Education was underway in Delhi, and although forty children had been selected to participate, Om Prakash was visiting his parents at the time and so was not asked to attend. When he found out about it, he decided to go to the Congress by bicycle. Om Prakash undertook a thirty-six hour bike ride to give an impressive statement about child labor to the Congress.

One year later, at age fourteen, Om Prakash was honored with the world's most prestigious award for children – the International Children's Peace Prize.

Launched in conjunction with Nobel Peace Prize Laureates, the honor includes a monetary award of $100,000 to be used by a children's project. The exceptional teenager traveled to the Netherlands to personally receive his award from former South African President F.W. DeKlerk. "I will work to support the families of child labourers," Om Prakash said, "so that the children can go to school and enjoy their childhood."[lxxxix]

lxv Human Rights Watch. Hidden Apartheid: Caste Discrimination against India's "Untouchables." 2006.

lxvi The Global March Against Child Labor, "Children Cost Less than Cattle," March 22, 2007.

lxvii UNICEF website, "The Picture in India," May 14, 2007. http://www.unicef.org/india/child_protection_152.htm.

lxviii Human Rights Watch, The Small Hands of Slavery - Bonded Child Labor in India. 1996.

lxix The Global March Against Child Labor, "Report on the Worst Forms of Child Labour." June 1998.

lxx Human Rights Watch, The Small Hands of Slavery - Bonded Child Labor in India. 1996.

lxxi Human Rights Watch. Hidden Apartheid: Caste Discrimination against India's "Untouchables." 2006.

lxxii Human Rights Watch, Small Change: Bonded Child Labor in India's Silk Industry. January 1, 2003.

lxxiii We Wish to Inform You That Tomorrow We Will be Killed With Our Families, Philip Gourevitch, Picador New York: 1998.

lxxiv U.S. Department of Labor, Bureau of International Labor Affairs, "Leather Footwear," accessed September 20, 2007, http://www.dol.gov/ilab/media/reports/iclp/sweat4/leather.htm

lxxv Hindustan Times, "Home to the second largest child population globally, India is the worldh sixth most dangerous place for children. They also constitute 40 per cent of human trafficking victims," October 22, 2007.

lxxvi Human Rights Watch, The Small Hands of Slavery - Bonded Child Labor in India. 1996.

lxxvii Embassy of India, Policy Statements, Washington D.C.

lxxviii International Herald Tribune, "Children's domestic labor resists India's legal efforts" by Amelia Gentleman. February 18, 2007.

lxxix BBC News, "Child Workers Face Uncertain Future" by Geeta Pandey. Oct. 9, 2006.

lxxx BBC News, "Child Workers Face Uncertain Future" by Geeta Pandey. Oct. 9, 2006.

lxxxi BBC News, "Child Workers Face Uncertain Future" by Geeta Pandey. Oct. 9, 2006.

lxxxii UNICEF, The State of the World's Children 2006.

lxxxiii Save The Children UK, Abuse Among Child Domestic Workers, Aug. 25, 2006.

lxxxiv Hindustan Times, "Nearly 70% child workers in West Bengal face physical abuse" by Romita Datta. May 11, 2007.

lxxxv InfoChange India, "Orissa's child domestic workers: The 'nowhere' children" by Manipadma Jena. July 2004.

lxxxvi The Hindu, "THE OTHER HALF: Death of a 10-year-old" by Kalpana Sharma. Sept. 7, 2006.

lxxxvii Global March Against Child Labor Blog: kNOw Child Labour 2 NO child labour. May 23, 2007.

lxxxviii UNICEF, The State of the World's Children 2006.

lxxxix The Hindu, "On a Mission Against Bondage" by Madhur Tankha, Nov. 23, 2006.

"What difference does it make to the dead, the orphans and the homeless, whether the mad destruction is wrought under the name of totalitarianism or the holy name of liberty or democracy?"

–*Mahatma Gandhi*

India's New Untouchables

I was making my way across India for a month, my final
destination the Miracle Foundation homes in Orissa where I
would spend the last ten days. Between Mumbai on the
southwest coast where I landed and Orissa in the east,
however, laid the state of Andhra Pradesh – the epicenter of
India's AIDS outbreak with the highest infection rates in the
country.

Most people are surprised to learn that India is one of
the countries with the largest HIV-positive population in
the world. In May 2006, The Joint United Nations
Programme on HIV/AIDS (UNAIDS) reported that there
were more people with HIV in India than any other country
in the world with 5.7 million infected. However, the
National AIDS Control Organization (NACO) disputed this
estimate, claiming that the actual figure was lower.[xc] The
contradiction was attributed to errors in the calculation

methods used. In 2007, using an expanded surveillance system and a revised and enhanced methodology, UNAIDS and NACO agreed on a new estimate for India – between two million and three-point-six million people living with HIV, putting India just behind South Africa and Nigeria in infections of the epidemic.[xci] Like sub-Saharan Africa in the last two decades, India is on the cusp of a burgeoning AIDS crisis.

The disease is silently spreading and reaching critical proportions. Almost one percent of people in the country's six most populous states are HIV-positive, and twenty out of thirty-seven states show high prevalence areas.[xcii] Although one percent may sound low, the sheer size of India's population – more than one billion – would make a widespread AIDS pandemic devastating. The one percentage figure is deeply disturbing to health officials because it is regarded as the tipping point, at which a smoldering health crisis can explode into an epidemic of vast magnitude.

In the western world, widely available medicines have slowed the progression of HIV and contributed to a dramatic decline in mortality, creating a common misperception that AIDS is waning. Nothing could be further from the truth. Every single day almost three times as many people die of AIDS in developing countries as died in the World Trade Center on 9/11. The epidemic has created a secondary human rights crisis – the orphaning of children on a massive scale. UNAIDS reports, "Orphaning remains the most visible, extensive, and measurable impact of AIDS on children."[xciii] Each day brings fifteen thousand new infections – and one in four of those are Indian.

After the tsunami hit South Asia in December 2004, there was a worldwide outpouring of assistance, donations and money. The response was tremendous, and rightly so in the face of such a catastrophe. Yet every two weeks, the same number of Indians die of AIDS as perished in the tsunami. No disaster is declared for these victims.

* * *

In mid March on my way northeast I flew into Chennai, the large city formerly known as Madras at the northern tip of Tamil Nadu state. Here I would connect with Caroline and Manjeet who were visiting an orphanage that The Miracle Foundation was considering supporting. From there we would make our separate ways to the home that Manjeet ran in Rourkela, he and Caroline going straight there and me following after spending the week in Andhra Pradesh, trying to learn more about the country's AIDS problem and how it was affecting children.

Chennai had the distinction of being the place where India's first AIDS case was detected, in a 1986 blood test procedure on prostitutes. It wasn't long before the infection began appearing in children. By 1993 an orphanage in Chennai had identified two HIV-positive children who were quickly transferred to a government hospital.[xciv] The children fell under the care of Dr. Pinagapany Manorama, the first female pediatric gastroenterologist in southern India and a former student of Dr. Suniti Solomon, the physician who had diagnosed the first AIDS patients.

I contacted Dr. Manorama about my research for this book and my itinerary through Chennai, and she eagerly agreed to talk to me about those early days in India's history of AIDS and its progression since then. Three hours after my plane landed, I was in the small office above her clinic. Pictures drawn by child patients lined the walls, and a furry red Elmo doll hung from one corner of a bulletin board. A thick, black daily planner notebook sat on the glass-top desk, bulging with papers and notes that evidenced a busy life. Dr. Manorama lowered herself into the rolling chair behind her desk, leaning against a Teenage Mutant Ninja Turtle pillow propped against the seat back for support.

It was easy to see how children would feel at ease with this doctor. She was a comfortingly plump woman, round and soft, with a sparkling crystal bindi above liquid brown eyes. She wore a simple gold chain around her neck and each wrist, and a light yellowish-green sari trimmed in gold. It could be said that Dr. Manorama had a grandmotherly air about her, except that she seemed too young for grandmother age.

She settled into an immediate description of those first two HIV-positive children she began treating nearly fifteen years ago. "Right away, I noticed the stigma the children faced as carriers of what was called the 'ghost disease.'" When she arrived to treat the small patients, Dr. Manorama found the hospital had isolated them in the farthest corners of the ward, by the toilets, and most of the staff refused to care for them. "People came to stare at them, like a circus sideshow, to see what children infected with this dreaded disease looked like."

When the hospital was ready to discharge the children there was no place for them to go. The orphanage where they had been living worried that the infection would spread to other children and refused to take them back. In the end, Dr. Manorama admitted them into her own private practice clinic.

"When we took the children in, we thought that they would die soon," she said bluntly. The five-year-old girl was already in a mental state of dementia and the three-year-old boy did not speak at all. Surprisingly, under the care of clinic staff the children started improving. "Within six months, their health was much better," Dr. Manorama said. "We began to realize that we were dealing with a disease which can be managed, if not cured."

Word of the doctor's success with these patients, and her willingness to take them in, spread throughout Chennai and eventually changed the course of her life and career. Soon more children were brought to the clinic, and then HIV-positive women and sex workers began coming. The doctor formed an NGO, Community Health Education Society (CHES), and opened the CHES Home for children infected or affected by HIV, financed by her own income from the private clinic. The women who came to the clinic were trained to be caregivers for the children. The government welfare office began partnering with CHES in 2005 to identify HIV-positive orphans anywhere in the state of Tamil Nadu and bring them to the home. By 2007 CHES was caring for forty-three children with plans to double capacity within a year. They began seeing successes such as local women stepping forward to foster and even adopt these children who belonged to no one.

Discrimination remained a constant challenge though, and Dr. Manorama even faced disapproval on a personal basis for her choice of work. There were those who felt she should be enjoying the income and lifestyle befitting a medical doctor with her training and reputation, instead of throwing away every opportunity for a prosperous life far from suffering and death. "But you know, I am caring for children. I will not leave my children," she avowed vehemently. "You have to be a loudspeaker for children, because they can't speak for themselves. I feel I have to speak for them."

It is clear that someone must. In addition to threatening their very survival, the stain of AIDS marks its victims like a scarlet letter, leaving them completely vulnerable to abuse and exploitation – a reality not only for those actually infected, but for family members and children orphaned by the disease. A Human Rights Watch investigation uncovered discrimination on a constant basis: segregation and expulsion from schools, refusal of treatment by doctors, rejection from orphanages and even their own family homes.[xcv] Sixty years after the caste system was officially abolished, they are India's new untouchables.

"Children are being turned away from schools, clinics and orphanages because they or their family members are

HIV-positive," reported Zama Coursen-Neff, a senior researcher with Human Rights Watch. "If the Indian government is serious about fighting the country's AIDS epidemic, it should stop ignoring children affected by AIDS and start protecting them from abuse."

In 2003 a six-year-old girl called Anu was sent home from kindergarten by her teacher in Maharashtra state. Her grandfather, who had been caring for Anu and her siblings after their parents died of AIDS, explained, "The teacher didn't allow her to come to school because she believes Anu is HIV-positive." The family doctor, Anu's own great-uncle, told him not to bring the girl to his clinic "because if you do, other people won't come."[xcvi]

In Gujarat state in October 2006, two HIV-positive boys were forced to leave the Jeevan Prabhat orphanage where they had lived for four years after staff said they posed an unacceptable risk to the safety of other children. Two months later, five HIV-positive children were expelled from a school in Kerala under pressure from parents who threatened to withdraw their children if the infected students did not leave – in spite of the state's policy that children with HIV/AIDS cannot be denied access to schools.[xcvii]

It took Dr. Manorama six years of work and sensitivity training before Chennai schools would accept the CHES children. "Through small steps, one school at a time, we made headway," she said. "At every level, we have to fight and convince."

Dr. Manorama's mentor who detected the first AIDS

case, Dr. Solomon, regrets to this day that it was diagnosed in the sex worker population. "I think if we had found HIV in a baby first, rather than streetwalkers, maybe we wouldn't have so much stigma," she told USA Today in a 2005 interview.[xcviii] I immediately related this to the history of AIDS in my own country – that if the disease had not shown up first in the gay population, then maybe *we* would have cared more. Perhaps even have done more about it, before two decades and millions of lives were gone.

I turned back to Dr. Manorama. "And what happened to those first two children you began treating in 1993?"

"The girl, she died when she was fifteen," the doctor said – before Anti-Retroviral Treatment, the medications that inhibit the replication of HIV, were available in any meaningful way in India. Recently, ART therapy has become more available for the other children, including the boy from the original two patients. At nearly fourteen years old, he was "doing okay," said Dr. Manorama. "We used to lose children in batches, sometimes five or six together. But since 2004, only one child has died."

* * *

The day after my visit with Dr. Manorama, I was to join Caroline and Manjeet for dinner before we all left Chennai. I also had plans to meet C. Prasanna Kumar, a man heavily involved in the struggle against AIDS some seventy-five miles north of Chennai. I had learned of Mr. Kumar's work through the Global Giving network as I researched from my home in Austin, and we had been communicating via phone and email for some months. Known as C.P., he ran a nonprofit organization called Health Education And Rural Training Society (HEARTS) which had provided the first HIV/AIDS awareness training in Andhra Pradesh in 2001. The training was conducted in partnership with the Peer Education Program of Los Angeles and attracted two hundred eighty participants comprised of teachers, social workers and teen groups. C.P. later established a home he called Little Hearts, where twenty-five children who have lost one or both parents to AIDS live.

C.P. had traveled to Chennai with his best friend, Anil, to escort me by train to visit the Little Hearts home. The two men arrived in the lobby of my hotel and walked past the reception desk slowly, gazing around the modern lobby in awe. C.P. was almost exactly my age, forty, of average height and build with a thick black mustache. When he spotted me waiting for him, he broke into a huge grin and rushed to clasp both my hands tightly.

"I have never been in a place such as this!" he exclaimed. One of the trendy, contemporary Park chain of boutique hotels, the Park Chennai was much fancier than the homestays and small inns I usually booked. However, I found a great deal online that had put the Park squarely at the lower end of the budget. I had also been a little nonplussed at its opulence on my arrival, so I could only imagine the lens through which C.P. and Anil viewed it and was strangely embarrassed.

I had invited the men to go with me to the group dinner that had been arranged. From the street, we caught a motorized rickshaw to the restaurant where Caroline and Manjeet were deep in conversation with an older Indian couple as they waited for us. Anil and C.P. seemed nervous and a bit intimidated as we approached the group.

"Manjeet!" I had not seen him since he had visited the Miracle Foundation in Austin the previous summer and threw my arms around him in a hug, completely forgetting what Caroline had told me about his discomfort with physical contact from unrelated women. Nevertheless, he patted my arm and seemed happy to see me. I hugged Caroline and introduced C.P. and Anil, as she introduced her friends, Mr. and Mrs. Srinivasan.

The Srinivasans were parents of a Miracle Foundation board member and originally from Andhra Pradesh, so they spoke C.P.'s local dialect. Later C.P. told me, "When Mrs. Srinivasan started speaking in Telugu, we felt very happy." He seemed to relax then, losing some of his self-consciousness. The teasing banter thrown around the table also helped lighten the mood.

"Why do you wear that brown turban?" Caroline asked Manjeet. "It just doesn't do anything for you. It's not a good color on you; you should wear the blue one."

Manjeet merely gazed at her calmly. "And why do you wear such lipstick?" he retorted. "It's far too bright, it makes you look too loud."

I laughed and Caroline turned to me. "You see how mean he is to me?" she said. "He's like my annoying older brother."

"I think you started it," I reminded her. Manjeet turned

to engage C.P. in conversation, and we all enjoyed an easy, friendly dinner before going our separate ways.

* * *

How do you explain love? How do you begin to describe and comprehend the forces of compassion, faith and dedication that can so define a person that he will spend the hours of his life loving those whom no else stops to notice? Those whom he has no obligation to care about, no reason to work for, and no reward other than the knowledge that he is making some small dent in the endless tide of need. The best you can hope to do is to stand outside a small, nondescript building on a dusty street in the middle of India, and watch two dozen once-homeless children rush out to greet the man who didn't allow them to fall through the crack.

Arriving with C.P. at the Little Hearts home, I was immediately given a tour by the entire household. It didn't take long. The place was so tiny, the size of a small one-bedroom apartment, that I could not imagine how twenty-five children and a few staff members slept there. There were two small rooms – the boys slept on the floor of one and girls in the other. Next was a broom closet kitchen barely big enough for two people to stand in, and bathrooms on the rooftop completed the structure. The back "play yard" consisted of a small patch of red dirt. The entire place could fit into the living room and office of my house – which at twelve hundred-fifty square feet is modest by U.S. standards.

Yet the children living there seemed happy to have a home, with little reference point to the cramped and bleak shelter in their completely healthy self-centeredness of childhood. They were well dressed, well fed and cared for. A thick garland of jasmine and marigold flowers was placed around my neck and the girls and boys lined up in separate groups in front of us on the floor. They stood one at a time to state their names, ages and level in school, then recited their ABCs as a group and sang. The blue walls were covered with pictures of animals, flowers and objects with the vocabulary words printed carefully in English. A world map and chalkboard were spread wide behind me.

For hours we played games and sang songs. Eager students brought me their schoolwork and stood by, nervously and proudly, as I pored over it. One boy of about ten with intense eyes and a mere wisp of a smile handed me an extraordinary science notebook. It was filled with intricate drawings of scientific experiments complete with hypotheses, notes, procedures and results, most of which I could not understand due to their complexity.

Most of the children were very young, ranging from four to ten years old, with only a couple of twelve or fourteen. The oldest was an eighth-grade girl called Sutrasini. When she wasn't playing chess she followed me quietly, watching with the interest an almost-adult exhibits in the actions of a grown-up. She was a serious girl who seemed to be drawn to someone older who she could try and relate to. I asked her questions about herself and her life at Little Hearts. Used to an everyday existence spent with these small children, Sutrasini yearned for someone to take her seriously, to recognize her maturity and intelligence as the young woman she was on the verge of becoming.

Sutrasini and the others attended school right down the street, and C.P. and his wife Mamatha - along with their own two sons, Prince and Boon - provided a loving surrogate family. Little Hearts was truly a place for children who had nowhere else to go. They were all HIV-negative; C.P. was not equipped medically or financially to take in HIV-positive children, who were sent to a government rehabilitation home. Often a teacher or other local official would bring a child to Little Hearts; in other cases C.P. heard of situations in the local community and offered to take in the orphans.

Their stories were heartbreaking. In early 2003, he read about an infant who had been abandoned in a nearby village after her fourteen-year-old mother was gang-raped. The mother disappeared after the attack, leaving her tiny daughter behind. A local teacher brought the infant, Anantha, to Little Hearts. Four years later, Anantha was a healthy, chubby-cheeked girl in a frilly yellow dress whom I could entertain for hours with hand-clapping games. She didn't tire of them until dark had long fallen and her eyes drooped sleepily.

C.P.'s wife, Mamatha, and I took the youngest group, including Anantha, into the small room to put them to bed on thin bedrolls that covered the floor. We sat beside them and talked quietly as the children drifted off to sleep. Anantha craned her neck on the pillow and gazed at me somberly, a hand cradled beneath her cheek and eyes wide and unblinking. I felt that I was being appraised, that she could see all the way into me, and I hoped I measured up to whatever thoughts were in her mind.

* * *

"I am not such a deserving person as you," C.P. told me often. When we discussed hotels, trains or taxis he demurred about being important enough for first or second class. On our train ride from Chennai, he had leaned over and confided that it was his first time to ride in an air-conditioned railway car. He had never been on an airplane in his life, he added. In fact, he had never been out of his state of Andhra Pradesh or its neighboring state, Tamil Nadu. In our email exchanges over previous months he fretted about his English, which was excellent, and agonized over a letter he was writing to Dr. Manjeet Pardesi, worried that his grammar and vocabulary weren't impressive enough. He had seemed reluctant to be included at dinner with "truly important" people such as Dr. Pardesi and the Srinivasans. "I am not such a deserving person," he repeated.

This was completely baffling to me. Here was a man who had dedicated his life to providing a home for kids he could hardly afford to care for, taking them into his own family. All around him, children's parents were dying, they were being kicked out of orphanages and schools and shunned by villages, and C.P. was often the only one there for them. What was most amazing was that he did not do this as his job, because it was required of him – he did it in addition to a regular full-time position as a government public relations officer. Not only did C.P. not get paid for his work under HEARTS, but he and Mamatha had poured their own money into the organization and gone into personal debt to carry on their mission.

C.P.'s idea of who was "deserving" was a paradox to me. I was only there to give witness to his incredible work for a few days, to write about it so that perhaps others would take up the cause. I was merely a spectator, a recorder, watching while he worked tirelessly to provide a new life for dozens of children.

HEARTS receives no government funding or support of any kind – like many others, C.P. recounted tales of pervasive corruption and bribery that run deep in the government. He said that many grants go to "shell" NGOs that funnel the money off and do not use it for what they say they will. Most government officials require a bribe to administer the funding and often report a higher number of children than are actually being served by the recipient organization, leaving the excess money to be split between the official and the NGO. "There is no accountability," C.P. said, "but who will question them?"

Every day he poured through local newspapers for stories of orphaned or abandoned children. Sadly, they appeared all too frequently. In Nellore District, a city of approximately 375,000 surrounded by twelve hundred villages and hamlets, one out of every ten people is a child under six years old and increasingly, the culprit of these children's lives is AIDS. C.P. would like to start a new campus that can accept HIV-positive children, but he would need far more funding than he currently receives from his one donor, The River Fund of Florida who supports HEARTS with approximately $460 per month. "If we have sufficient support, we can do miracles here," he declared.

We were sitting on the roof of the Little Hearts building, C.P. reading me newspaper stories of children left alone. There were many, each more agonizing than the last. One article appeared under the headline "How Long This Darkness?" Three brothers had recently lost their parents to AIDS and had only an elderly grandfather left to support them. The grandfather used to work as a field laborer, but that income was not enough to support three growing boys and he began to supplement his meager salary by begging. Local villages refused to take them in. The reporter ended the article by urging the government and NGOs to come forward and help them. When C.P. called about the children, he was told that he was the only person who had.

I asked C.P. how he could possibly accept the three boys – he was already well past capacity with the twenty-five children living at Little HEARTS. He gazed back at me for a long moment of silence before answering, "If not me, who? If not now, when?"

* * *

There are nearly two million such children in India who have lost their parents to AIDS. It is the most AIDS orphans in any single country of the world, and their numbers are

expected to double within the next five years.[xcix] More
children are living now with HIV-positive parents than
have already been orphaned.[c] A village near Little Hearts
home called Cherlopalem was one of many places where
this was happening before my very eyes. Cherlopalem was
a small farming community of thirty families of Dalits, the
lower caste formerly known as "untouchables."

By spring 2007, however, the lush green fields
surrounding the village stood empty. Three-fourths of its
residents had been affected by AIDS, leaving almost no one
to work the crops. The decimation of this village was so
complete that local newspapers and television stations
covered it. On April 8, 2007 the *Eenadu* newspaper reported,
"The village, known for its hardworking lifestyle, is now
ravaged by a cureless malady. AIDS has become a
nightmare for this colony." [ci] Seven people had died of the
disease within eight months and dozens more were in the
last stages, "living like corpses" as the reporter described.
One infected woman who had been shown on a television
newscast was so shamed by the exposure that she
subsequently stopped eating and taking her medications,
and soon died.

One of the most noticeable things in Cherlopalem was
what was missing. There were virtually no middle-aged
people. The small community now almost entirely consisted
of the elderly and children, some of whom had left school to
work as day laborers, while others roamed the village
without direction. As the leading cause of death worldwide
for people ages fifteen to forty-nine – the very ages at which

many people are raising families – AIDS is an epidemic that
wipes out the middle-aged population and results in the
very old taking care of the very young, as well as the other
way around.[cii] As it devastates this generation, it leaves
hundreds of thousands of children in its wake.

C.P. Kumar took upon himself the Herculean task of
tracking the orphaned children of Cherlopalem and trying
to provide some type of home or assistance for them. When
he visited the village, the residents were initially reluctant
to talk with him. By then, they had learned the lessons of
prejudice, ridicule and shame that came with the disease.
After slowly gaining their trust in the fact that he was only
there to help, people began telling C.P. their own stories as
well as similar situations in nearby villages. He visited these
communities too, including one called Kovur where
seventy-five HIV/AIDS patients met with him. World
Vision had recently closed their Kovur project that had
supplied food, medicine and school fees to over four
hundred HIV-positive residents and their children.

After twelve years of the World Vision program,
funding had run out. In response to my inquiry, World
Vision Media Director Jayanth Vincent wrote, "We know
that the issue of HIV and AIDS, especially those affecting
children, are high in this area and so we have been
exploring funding options to continue the HIV and AIDS
interventions in Nellore."

A dozen grandparents begged for Little Hearts to take
in their grandchildren; then twenty more; then another
thirty. Soon C.P. had collected information and medical

reports on nearly one hundred local children whose parents had either died or were dying of AIDS and had no one willing to care for them. One afternoon a young woman, Jyothi, called C.P. on the phone after learning of his visit to her village. Jyothi had contracted HIV from her husband, who worked as a cook in a hotel one hundred kilometers away. They had both been receiving medical treatments and food from World Vision before its program ended. Jyothi's husband had since grown so ill that he was no longer able to work. On the telephone Joythi wept to C.P., requesting food and medicine, and begged him to take her four year old son to live at Little Hearts home.

These villages are located just north of the national highway, which has contributed significantly to the spread of the disease and caused the state of Andhra Pradesh to be known as the "hot zone" of the epidemic. The national highways between New Delhi, Calcutta, Chennai and Mumbai run through at least six districts where HIV prevalence is above 2.5 percent – including Andhra Pradesh, where these highways converge. Traveling them reveals a country's secret sex life, and the potent mix of denial and discrimination that keeps the epidemic under wraps. The nation's three million truck drivers, of whom as many as twenty percent are HIV-positive, patronize the red light districts at such junctures and then carry the infection along.[ciii] Migratory workers play a part as well, traveling to find work and often living away from their families for months at a time. The map of HIV prevalence in India reads almost like a map of highways such as the one running nearby Cherlopalem.

The *Eenadu* reported that locals considered the husbands to be the perpetrators of the disease and questioned if the high rate of illiteracy was a contributing factor. "None of the villagers have a good understanding of the disease," the article stated. "No one knows how it spreads or what precautions to take." The remaining residents confessed that they knew nothing about the "dreaded disease." This complete lack of information was illustrated in a 2005-2006 National Health Survey which found that only eighty percent of men and fifty-seven percent of women aged fifteen to forty-nine had even heard of AIDS, and that condom use was about five percent.[civ] It's a common belief in many parts of India that if you touch a person with HIV/AIDS or share a meal you will become infected.

Such fears and myths surrounding the disease are shocking, and the sexually conservative society makes education and awareness efforts challenging. The push to keep the topic taboo means that many teachers, government officials and doctors still don't know the basic facts about HIV transmission, much less the general population. There have been numerous reports of violence and harassment against social workers who provide information and hand out condoms – even abuse by police. The medical community often refuses to deliver babies of HIV-positive women, and fewer than half of all secondary schools offer any AIDS education. Explicit, factual information about HIV transmission and how to prevent it is almost nonexistent, and so the disease continues its deadly reach into communities and families.

Cherlopalem provides a microcosm of the ability of AIDS to unravel the social fabric of entire communities. Village after village of elderly people and children left behind, working to survive together, in the wake of AIDS' senseless wasting of the generation between them. These families and children are bearing the brunt of what is widely considered the greatest humanitarian crisis of our time.

---

xc NACO, HIV/AIDS epidemiological Surveillance & Estimation report for the year 2005, April 2006.

xci UNAIDS, NACO and WHO, "2.5 Million People in India Living with HIV, According to New Estimates," July 6, 2007.

xcii The Indian Express, November 20, 2006.

xciii UNAIDS, UNICEF and USAID, Children on the Brink, 2004.

xciv Dr. P. Manorama, Personal Interview, March 16, 2007, Chennai.

xcv Human Rights Watch, Future Forsaken, 2004.

Human Rights Watch, Future Forsaken, 2004.

xcvii India eNews, "Another Kerala school ousts five HIV children," Sept. 7, 2006
http://www.indiaenews.com/education/20061207/31627.htm.

xcviii USA Today, Steve Sternberg, February 23, 2005.

xcix World Bank, At-A-Glance India: AIDS and Orphans.

c Vasavya Mahila Mandali in collaboration with the International HIV/AIDS Alliance, "Moving Forward: A Report on Pioneering Responses to Children Affected by HIV/AIDS in Andhra Pradesh, India." 2004.

ci The Eenadu, "Death Bells in That Dalit Colony," April 8, 2007, translated by Manoj Nagulapally.

cii UNAIDS, UNICEF and USAID, Children on the Brink, 2004.

ciii The New Yorker, "India's Plague" by Michael Specter, December 17, 2001.

civ National Family Health Survey: http://nfhsindia.org/nfhs3.html.

"Pity may represent little more than the impersonal concern which prompts the mailing of a check, but true sympathy is the personal concern which demands the giving of one's soul."

–*Martin Luther King, Jr.*

The Children Left Behind

Imagine you are a twelve-year-old boy. You live in India, on the outskirts of a city called Vijayawada. Your name is Yesu Babu.

Your home is a tiny two-room concrete block, approximately two hundred square feet, in a slum known as the Vambay Colony. Imagine that you share this small home with your grandmother, Durgamma, and your nine-year-old brother. You live with your grandmother because your parents died of AIDS – first your father, who brought the infection home, in 2001; then your mother followed in 2004. There was no one left to take care of you and your brother except your elderly grandmother, who never expected to be raising children again.

Soon you learn that although you are HIV-negative, your young brother is HIV-positive. He begins to grow ill.

He battles many infections. He cries in the night when he's sick and calls for his mother.

Almost crippled with severe joint pain, your grandmother can barely walk and cannot physically work. Even if she could, someone has to care for your brother. There is no one else to provide an income for this new family that has formed. So, you let your brother go to school, although his future is painfully uncertain, while you work. You leave home for a week at a time to travel for migrant construction or agricultural jobs. You are paid thirty to fifty rupees per day – roughly a dollar or less.

You are just a boy. You know you should be in school. You should have a childhood, but it has been traded in far too soon for adult work and worries, for hardships that no twelve-year-old should ever have to face. But what can you do? There is no one else. There is no other way. From a normal life with a mother and father, school, a childhood, possibilities – to this previously unimagined reality.

This is your new normal.

* * *

What was happening to the families of Cherlopalem was happening in hundreds of towns and villages across India in a slow, silent obliteration. I met Yesu's family after I left Little Hearts home and traveled on north, through Vijayawada on my way to join back up with Caroline and Manjeet. Vasavya Mahila Mandali (VMM), a community-based HIV/AIDS support program that focuses on women and children, works in Vambay Colony where Yesu lives and took me to the slum to meet many such families living in the shadow of AIDS.

As we drove past the outskirts of Vijayawada, a city of about a million people close to the Bay of Bengal on the eastern coast of India, Abraham Mutluri explained how Vambay Colony sprung up two and a half years ago, almost overnight. Abraham was a Programme Coordinator with VMM who had been doing outreach in Vambay for two years, providing medical care and support for HIV-positive people and working to reduce the stigma of AIDS.

"Thousands of people from surrounding rural villages migrated to Vijayawada for work and began setting up flimsy households along the canals," said Abraham. Soon the government built eight thousand of the small concrete boxes like the one Durgamma and her two grandsons lived in, right next to each other in row after endless row. In a plan designed to make the city of Vijayawada "slumless," occupants of the city's slums were moved to Vambay as well with promises of better housing. Instead, the relocated residents found themselves in a much worse situation – not only did they now have to travel a long way to reach jobs in the city, but they faced even poorer living conditions in Vambay, which lacked adequate water, septic systems and drainage. The Hindu newspaper reported that the "beneficiaries" had simply been relocated from a slum of thatched houses to a concrete slum.

The article also charged that many of the homes had not gone to their designated recipients, but instead were allotted to friends of government leaders. More than fifteen hundred homes stood empty, despite a waiting list of over two hundred families who had already paid the required five thousand rupees. For families who had moved in, ninety-five percent of the homes lacked proper bathrooms which were a promised component; while the toilets were provided, they were not properly connected to the septic tanks which soon began to overflow and back up into the ground where people tried to grow plants and children played. But the biggest problem the residents faced was a constant water shortage.[cv]

As soon as our car crossed the river and turned into the community, all of these problems were evident. Dusty, narrow lanes wound between concrete bunkers perhaps ten feet wide that lined the dirt roads without a break. Some of these homes had ladders propped in front of them, evidence that residents were attempting to expand their miniscule living quarters by taking advantage of the flat rooftop space. Overhead electrical wires criss-crossed and hung down haphazardly, trailing the ground in some places. Lines of clothing hung out to dry stretched between buildings, the faded fabrics flapping in the breeze above the weeds. In spots here and there flowers had been planted, small circles of hope where yellow marigolds and orange gladiolas fought for space in the rocky earth.

The car was parked and we got out, Abraham leading me to Yesu's home. The people were far less interested in this foreign visitor than anywhere else I had been in India, giving me no more than a cursory glance. They seemed too preoccupied with chores and tasks at hand, or simply too tired to care. The place was eerily quiet, no music or chattering, no cars beeping by.

There seemed no such thing as sanitation or hygiene in Vambay. The drains were choked and overflowing, a sure breeding ground for mosquitoes. Children squatted by the side of the road to defecate, and the air reeked of urine. Other children played with simple things on front stoops or in the small lanes – a dirty ball, two or three jacks, a piece of string. The homes were dark and poorly ventilated, no more than concrete lockers, each an arm's length from the next. In front of each doorway ran an open sewer which must be stepped over to enter the house. The flies were incredible, swarms of them everywhere, an incessant presence. Bowls of food and open bags of grain sat around, with no refrigeration and very little storage space. I thought of the flies and how they must land on both the sewers and the food.

We ducked through a piece of material strung across the front door of a house. It was dark inside, with two small beds pushed together in a T formation. A two-burner electric hotplate provided the only kitchen. Cooking utensils and clothing lined open shelves above one bed. On the other, Yesu's little brother Venugopal laid curled up with his back to us. Grandmother Durgamma invited me to sit on a red wooden stool with a gesture of her hand, and she crouched down next to me on the floor, her purple sari trailing in the dust that covered the concrete. Her face was deeply lined, the large gold ring in her nose flashing in contrast to the dark skin around it.

Sitting together in the cramped house, Durgamma spoke to me about her life as Abraham translated. "It is very hard taking care of my two grandchildren. I have leg pains and cannot play with them," she said. "I want to take care of them, but it is difficult. I don't need anything for myself. I am living only for my grandsons." She held her fingertips to her forehead and silver hair as she spoke. Her hands were like delicate parchment paper, dry and seemingly capable of flaking away at the slightest touch.

Her daughter, Yesu's and Venugopal's mother, did not reveal her illness until shortly before her death. Durgamma learned of Venugopal's HIV-positive status through a blood test. He was always tired because he had difficulty sleeping at night, and his grandmother worried about his constant eye infections. She was also concerned about Yesu, going off to work in construction at such a young age. "He has picked up some bad habits from the older boys at work," she said. Her brow was etched in a permanent expression of worry.

"I am only one. I am always thinking about their futures. I want to see them through to eighteen, but if something happens to me, what will become of them?" she asked. It was the same question in my mind as I glanced at the sleeping form of Venugopal, who made barely a lump on the bed next to me. Their situation seemed so tenuous, their survival entirely dependent on this hobbling old woman and a twelve-year-old boy.

The family's plight was an all-too-common legacy of India's exploding AIDS epidemic and a familiar story in Vambay Colony. The trend of grandparents raising grandchildren has become so prevalent – as many as forty percent of these orphans live with their grandparents[cvi] – that VMM and similar organizations started what they call "Granny Clubs." These are social and educational networks of women (and some men) like Durgamma who are caring for orphaned grandchildren. The granny clubs generally have ten to fifteen members who meet once a month, with social time and education about various topics. At one meeting, they might learn about HIV medications and treatment; at another, they might discuss nutrition.

The time is also used to make friendships, share problems, and offer solutions. "Sometimes we play games or sing," Durgamma told me about her club. "We have become friends, like sisters, and we support each other. We are older people who have watched our children die. We share our joys and our sorrows."

Ramulamma was another active granny club member in Vambay Colony. From Durgamma's house we drove to another side of the sprawling slum where we met her and her great-grandson Krishna. Ramulamma's granddaughter, Krishna's mother, also lived there but was at her job as a hotel maid in Vijayawada. The breadwinner of the family, she earned forty rupees per day – less than one U.S. dollar – although it cost ten rupees to travel into the city and back. This home was even poorer than the one I had just come from; instead of wooden beds with mattresses, I saw only a metal-frame cot bare of sheets or pillows. Water pots and cooking supplies sat directly on the otherwise bare floor. Little else filled the small structure.

We sat together on a thin beige quilt covering the floor. Ramulamma's face was also dark and lined and topped by a clump of thinning silver hair. Her bony, naked shoulder poked out of the blue and purple cotton sari draped around her, lacking even the blouse that was typically worn underneath the traditional garment. As she began to speak I could see that she had only one tooth.

They were a family with three generations affected by HIV: Krishna's father died two years ago, and his grandfather died just the month before, both from AIDS. Now Krishna was also HIV-positive. Like Durgamma, this grandmother was dry-eyed and matter of fact about their situation. In Vambay it seemed death was not a feared stranger but a constant, familiar companion. Tears were an indulgence these elders had neither the time nor the luxury for. In their daily scrabble for existence they could not afford to keep accounts of regret.

Krishna sat cross-legged on the floor facing me in his khaki shorts and sleeveless red sweater. The boy was so tiny I would have guessed him to be four or five years old; when I inquired I was told that he was nine. His eyes seemed too big for his face and he did not smile, watching me write down his medical history with little interest.

VMM provided doctor care and medicine every month for Krishna, as well as a local physician who was available for immediate needs; however he was not on Anti-Retroviral Treatment because he was not deemed sick enough. In India, CD4 blood count levels must be two hundred or below to qualify for ART drugs – the level at which HIV is medically considered to have become full-blown AIDS. Only seven percent of HIV-positive people were receiving any ART therapy in 2005.[cvii] In the United States, ART is started well before this time to *prevent* AIDS, generally at CD4 levels of three hundred to three hundred-fifty.[cviii] The World Health Organization asserts that antiretroviral therapy is a requirement for effective HIV/AIDS care, because without it life expectancy of those infected is short.[cix] Krishna continued to have regular blood tests so that ART drug treatment could be started as soon as his condition qualified. His small body was a battleground in which a war was being waged and AIDS was making its slow, inexorable victory.

Krishna and his grandmother gazed at me listlessly as we spoke, both with the same vacant eyes. In those two pairs of eyes laid a world of despair, devoid of any hopes or dreams. They waited patiently for my next inquiry. Abraham looked at me expectantly. I knew I was supposed to ask more questions, but I could think of no other words. Silence seemed to demand all the space between us. Everything I wanted to know was there in those eyes that stared back at me.

* * *

In spite of their hardships Krishna and Venugopal are among the more fortunate children living with HIV because they have family homes, however meager. Those without kinship ties – or whose families refuse to take them in – often end up in institutions, forming child-headed households, or simply on the streets. They are the missing face of AIDS, these children left behind.

Before Abraham and I drove out to Vambay Colony, I spent a couple of hours at the VMM office in Vijayawada, speaking with support manager Keerthi Bollineni and Dr. Deeksha Pillarisetty, Medical Director of VMM. The space was simple but clean and well-equipped; several staff members sat in the main room at computer terminals while I followed the two women into a private office. They looked like they could be sisters, with round faces and medium-length wavy hair held back in ponytails. We sat around a desk and Keerthi led me through a CD presentation of VMM's programs, which focus primarily on women and children through home-based medical care, support groups, mentoring programs and study/recreation centers. Dr. Pillarisetty fidgeted with her mobile phone while interjecting a passionate commentary.

"They are missing their entire childhoods," she said. "They go immediately into adulthood at a very young age." Becoming orphaned or sick themselves are not the only ways children are harmed by the epidemic. The impact on their emotional and psychological wellbeing is devastating. "The child-headed households are a particular concern," Dr. Pillarisetty continued, estimating that one-fourth of children affected by AIDS live in homes with no adult guardians present. Her eyes and voice filled with intensity, she leaned across the desk and described the trauma these children face alone.

"They are the most common caregivers for sick parents,

which impedes their education. Eventually they watch those parents die. And even then, because of the stigma, no one wants to touch them or take care of them." All too often these children must then step into adult roles as guardians of younger siblings or wage earners to support the remaining family. They may be denied their property and inheritance rights, face discrimination from neighbors, and deal with fears for their own health.

Alarming new evidence by UNAIDS found that orphans and children living outside family settings have a higher risk of exposure to HIV infection due to limited information about prevention, lack of role models and adult supervision, vulnerability to abuse and increased poverty.[cx] Girls are especially susceptible because they are more likely to be removed from school to care for sick parents or other family members, and are often the last in the family to receive medical care.[cxi] Less access to education, sexual abuse and child marriage all place girls at a higher possibility of becoming infected. Loss of family income can push them into the sex trade and lack of control over safe sex, even within marriage, puts them at a disadvantage. Many families marry daughters off at increasingly young ages so the girls will have someone to care for them after parental deaths. Parents also fear the risk of HIV will render their daughters unmarriageable, a finding corroborated by Human Rights Watch.[cxii]

This disturbing trend has the added effect of creating a lot of very young widows. "I see many girls widowed by the age of eighteen," said Dr. Pillarisetty, relating the story of one girl who was married at the age of thirteen, widowed at fourteen, and is now fifteen years old and living with HIV. Often these widows are blamed for the husband's infection and death, and outcast by his family.

India's crisis is acute in part because the government has done little to protect children affected by HIV/AIDS, and has no provisions for the orphaned. "The national and global response to the HIV/AIDS crisis in India has virtually ignored children," Keerthi said. "The strategy has focused primarily on high-risk target groups: the sex trade, truckers who spread the infection from town to town, and drug users." Eighty percent of AIDS funding goes toward prevention in the high-risk populations, and only twenty percent to caring for those living with HIV. But, the epidemic has been spreading so rapidly and for so many years that it has long since moved from these high-risk groups into the general population. Married women contract the disease from their husbands, who often bring it home from sex workers or other men. The strong cultural taboo against homosexuality means that gay men typically marry and have families, but continue sexual activity with other men outside of marriage. There is even a term for it – MSM, or men who have sex with men – and the concept of a homosexual identity is virtually nonexistent.

Tackling these issues means challenging long-held social attitudes to educate the general population about transmission and prevention, and will require an open and direct campaign by the media, government and societal leaders. AIDS awareness has yet to become a "cause" like in the west where it has received attention from celebrities and the media, although a few Bollywood stars and cricket players are beginning to lend their voices to the message. Initiatives like the Heroes Project, launched by Richard Gere and Parmeshwar Godrej, seek to reduce the both the spread of HIV/AIDS and discrimination surrounding it through national media campaigns, and by advocating for policy changes. Two representatives of Heroes Project spoke with me, confirming Keerthi Bollineni's charges of a grossly inadequate response to the epidemic.

"It is not a priority for the government," said Nidhi Dubey, Advocacy Director. "There are plenty of sex worker projects, or those working with the truckers, but hardly any projects reaching children. People believe it's mostly sex workers. There is a morality attached to it."

But the most vulnerable groups are young people and women, according to Executive Director Kanika Singh. "One out of every three people infected with HIV is a woman, and eighty percent of these women are housewives. Mothers unknowingly pass on the infection to their children." Mother to child transmission is the most common source of infection in children, at a rate of thirty thousand per year,[cxiii] but children are also acquiring HIV through blood transfusions, syringe injections, and consensual or non-consensual sexual contact.[cxiv]

Yet, Kanika added, "Nobody talks about HIV-positive children. A focus on children could motivate the awareness campaign and mobilize the general population." Too often success with awareness is translated into numbers of people who have simply heard about AIDS, but true education and prevention means knowing how it actually transmits and how to protect oneself.

"We need a simple but very integrated approach in the schools with sexual health and education programs," said Nidhi. "It has to be something where you reach out to teachers, parents, the larger community." Three months after we spoke, several states enacted a ban against all sex education in schools, a troubling step backwards in the fight against the epidemic.[cxv]

Without explicit awareness and education efforts on a massive scale, the number of infections will grow larger while treatment efforts chase them. Prevention in the general population is key on a simple mathematical basis if nothing else – it makes far more sense to provide the necessary tools to avoid more infections than face a crisis that has grown tenfold years down the road. The lessons of Africa have taught us that. Avoiding the controversy of open discussions, particularly among young people, about sex, condoms, prostitution, homosexuality and other sensitive topics will merely magnify the devastation in years to come.

"Richard [Gere] believes the window where we can make a difference on HIV/AIDS is short, and it's now," Kanika Singh said. "If we don't act now, it may be too late." The possibility of action coming too late is an alert also sounded by Dr. Richard Feachem of the Global Fund to Fight AIDS. In a Science Magazine special report on AIDS in India, Feachem argued that India is the most important milestone worldwide. "If we lose the fight in India, we lose the fight globally," he warned.[cxvi]

While the country has not been in complete denial over the looming disaster, government has consistently minimized it in the shadow of its new prosperity and growing middle class. Ironically, the explosion of India onto the world market and its resulting affluence have correlated to the increasing epidemic through huge migratory trends and loss of extended family connections.[cxvii] Officials downplayed the numbers of affected children over and over to Human Rights Watch investigators, saying either they "can't get the figures" or the problems had been overstated with too much publicity. Some government representatives asserted that there were no HIV-positive children in their schools or institutions, in spite of statistics to the contrary, and most acknowledged they had no programs for the care and support of these children.[cxviii]

Resources for children affected by the disease have increased in recent years, but funding is nevertheless small in comparison to the overall HIV/AIDS budget, which is itself woefully inadequate. Compared to almost $20 billion in the U.S., India's total funding for HIV/AIDS was $103 million for 2005-2006[cxix] - ten cents per person – although a fivefold increase to $2.6 billion has been proposed.[cxx] An enormous gap exists between what is needed and what is actually being done to address the needs of these children.

Small strides are being made. On World AIDS Day in December 2006 the National Paediatric HIV/AIDS Initiative was launched, the first nationwide program to treat

children living with HIV/AIDS. In conjunction with the
Clinton Foundation, the initiative will provide free pediatric
dosages of anti-retroviral medicines to young children
living with the disease.[cxxi] The AIDS Prevention and Control
Project announced a new virtual training center in March
2007 for doctors who provide care to HIV/AIDS patients,[cxxii]
while at the same time the Tamil Nadu government
launched a free nutritional support program at ART
treatment centers.[cxxiii] A study released in early 2006
reported a fall in HIV-prevalence in southern India by one-
third, one of the best successes reported so far.[cxxiv]

Dr. Manorama confirmed that prevalence in Tamil
Nadu has declined from 1.1% to 0.5% over the last three to
four years. Countering this, however, is the fact that there
was no such decline in northern India, and some AIDS
activists question whether the lower figures take into
account the four hundred thousand AIDS-related deaths in
the same year – the highest in the world.[cxxv]

The National AIDS Control Programme recently
implemented the third phase of its plan to halt and reverse
the epidemic within five years by providing more ART
treatments. This is an encouraging step, but the focus
remains on high-risk groups such as commercial sex
workers and drug users. The plan calls for reaching ninety-
five percent of youth but does outline any specifics for
doing so, and by 2011 hopes to provide treatment to at least
thirty-nine thousand children and three hundred thousand
adults.[cxxvi] Considering that the current HIV infections in the

country are in the millions, those numbers hardly seem capable of halting the epidemic.

Poverty and lack of basic medical care are major obstacles in providing treatment. A large portion of the population still lacks access to simple necessities such as clean drinking water. There is not enough money in the skeletal public healthcare infrastructure to fight diseases that kill millions such as TB, malaria and simple diarrhea, much less treat AIDS – a disease present in one percent of the population or less, and for which there is no cure. Although more ART drugs are now being provided, HIV testing is not available free of charge. The drug regimens are costly and sometimes extremely complicated; if not completed properly they often make the illness worse. Patients also develop resistance to drugs, which can cause more harm than not having treatment at all. The cost of the nutritional program required and transportation to reach the treatment centers, especially from rural areas, is prohibitive for many – effectively putting such treatment beyond their reach.[cxxvii] Joanne Csete, Director of the HIV/AIDS program at Human Rights Watch, said, "It is a sad irony that India is one of the biggest producers of the drugs that have transformed the lives of people with AIDS in wealthy countries. But for millions of Indians, access to these medicines is a distant dream."[cxxviii]

With no real availability of treatment, there is little incentive to get tested. Without knowing if they are infected, sexual behaviors do not change. Fear of discrimination discourages people from doing anything that might label them HIV-positive, including protecting themselves, getting tested or seeking treatment. The U.S. Agency for International Development (USAID) estimates that an alarming ninety percent of those infected with HIV don't know about their status until a health crisis occurs.[cxxix] The result is that the epidemic is kept under cover where it can spread unchecked.

It is one of the major dilemmas of the Indian AIDS crisis – treatment versus prevention. Programs in other countries such as Thailand and Brazil have shown that dual approaches can work when implemented early and powerfully, even in areas of extreme poverty. While eradicating poverty is a worthy goal it can be concurrent with fighting AIDS successfully; as Bill Gates pointed out, the world didn't have to eliminate poverty before it was able to eliminate smallpox.[cxxx]

In the grip of such an epidemic, India cannot afford to make a choice between treating the disease and preventing it. The young generation who are today being orphaned by the thousands will soon grow up – and their potential impact on the epidemic as they become sexually active is a high area of concern. Missing family ties, they often form unhealthy attachments in which they are vulnerable to infection and abuse.

"They just want a relationship – it doesn't matter what kind it is," said Dr. Pillarisetty of VMM. "There is nobody for them, nobody wants them. They are very traumatized."

* * *

In Vambay Colony, Abraham and I had visited other families devastated by AIDS and sat in on a children's support group held in a small community center. With each story my insides grew tighter, until I sat on the floor of Ramulamma's bare, dusty house with the eyes of the old woman and her grandson Krishna heavy upon me. Their gazes felt glued to mine and I didn't want to leave them even when there were no more questions, nothing left to say.

But when Abraham stood and led me out of the small room, into the fading afternoon sun, and began telling me about the next family he planned for us to visit, I suddenly felt I had to leave. I asked if we could go back to Vijayawada instead.

"But, there are more people to talk to, and then a visit back at the office…" he began. I didn't want to seem uninterested or ungrateful – he and Keerthi and Dr. Pillarisetty were showing me what I had come to see – but I felt an almost overpowering urge to be alone.

"Please, I need to go back to the hotel," I pressed. "I need to do some writing from these notes while they're still fresh, and I'm so tired." So, we headed away from Vambay Colony.

These things were all true; we had been in the slum village for many hours and I was exhausted and hungry. But the real reasons I begged off from the remainder of Abraham's plans, I couldn't articulate to him. I simply could not absorb more. I felt weak and selfish and spoiled that I had a modest, but nice, hotel room to go back to; one in which I could bathe with hot water and where food would be delivered right to my door with a simple phone call.

Nonetheless, something inside me needed solitude. Needed to go through everything I had seen and heard so I could try to make sense of it, because it made no sense. How could this disease be a treatable, manageable illness for some and a death sentence for others? What needed to be done for Yesu and his HIV-positive brother, for Krishna, was so simple. In other places of the world, treatments were readily available and children did not lay in beds inside concrete lockers, wracked with AIDS. Because the disease disproportionately affects those already living without basic provisions of health care, education, and nutrition, it creates an apartheid between the rich and the poor. Lifesaving medicines were at the ready in India for those who could afford them.

It was not the drugs that were expensive – it was the patents. Indian law allowed companies to produce generic equivalents of drugs like AIDS antiretrovirals, making them much more accessible to the poor. Yet even at that moment, pharmaceutical giants like Novartis were challenging these intellectual property laws. They did not want drugs they sold for thousands of dollars available on the market for hundreds. They claimed that the patents were necessary to protect their research and to encourage future scientific and medical research. Yet, research and development accounts for only a small percentage of expenses, and is fully subsidized by domestic sales of routine medicines at higher retail prices – with substantial profits left over. In fact, drug company profits *after* research and development costs were more than double the profits of Fortune 500 companies.[cxxxi]

Many people question whether patents for such life-saving drugs, in light of the massive profits available through other, more commercial drugs, are ethical at all. Dr. Jonas Salk was of that belief and refused to patent his polio vaccine invention. "There is no patent," he said. "Could you patent the sun?" Yet in the pharmaceutical companies' quest to protect their products and profits at all costs, the lives of the abjectly poor in Vambay were of little worth. In a world where two different treatment regimens were available depending on wealth and geography, in which AIDS deaths had drastically fallen in western nations at the same time they were exploding in African and Asian countries, those dead parents were expendable.

They had not been expendable to Yesu and his brother, or to Krishna. A simple regimen of medicine and proper nutrition, an incredibly small amount of money, and lives in Vambay could be vastly different. It wouldn't take much, it was not an impossible or hopeless situation…but for those families, it might as well be, for these things were as out of reach as diamonds. And so they died, one at a time, while their children and elderly were left to take care of one another – including the sons and daughters who had inherited HIV from their parents in a wholly unnecessary legacy of destruction.

That we can know this and yet do nothing is, as Stephen Lewis of the United Nations put it, "mass murder by complacency."[cxxxii] We wonder why generations before us didn't speak up as entire peoples were kidnapped from their home countries and enslaved. We ask how the world could have stood by and allowed six million Jews to be exterminated in the Holocaust. How will we answer when our children ask what we did while millions were orphaned by AIDS?

If we fail in this battle, the face of the future lies in the eyes of Krishna and his grandmother. Their hopelessness seeped into me until I felt as though there was nothing beneath my feet. All that I had known before, all that had seemed true and solid, became as insubstantial as air. I fell into a deep silence and there was no safety or security because all around me was only an abyss. The second I broke away from their gazes my breath was shallow, my bones felt fragile, and I held my body tight and straight to keep it from collapsing. Simply put, my heart just couldn't take any more. The wrecked lives left in the wake of AIDS' destructive path had faces and stories, and their suffering knew my name. Those eyes will stay with me forever, I suspect.

---

cv The Hindu, "It's No Better with Vambay Houses," June 24, 2006.

cvi Kaveesher Krishnan, SAATHII, Personal interview March 21, 2007.

cvii UNAIDS, 2006 Report on the Global AIDS Epidemic, May 2006.

cviii Anjali Gopalan, Naz Foundation, Telephone Interview, April 22, 2007.

cix World Health Organization, Antiretroviral Therapy, http://www.who.int/hiv/topics/arv/en/index.html.

cx UNAIDS, UNICEF and USAID, Children on the Brink, 2004.

cxi Human Rights Watch, Future Forsaken, 2004.

cxii Human Rights Watch, Future Forsaken, 2004.

cxiii UNICEF, "Reducing Mother-to-Child Transmission of HIV/AIDS in India" – June 28 2005 http://www.unicef.org.nz/media/news/news1118808739.html.

cxiv Human Rights Watch, Future Forsaken, 2004.

cxv BBC News, "Indian State Bans Sex Education" by Monica Chadha. http://news.bbc.co.uk/2/hi/south_asia/6523371.stm.

cxvi Science Magazine, "HIV/AIDS: India's Many Epidemics" by Jon Cohen, April 23, 2004.

cxvii Vasavya Mahila Mandali in collaboration with the International HIV/AIDS Alliance, "Moving Forward: A Report on Pioneering Responses to Children Affected by HIV/AIDS in Andhra Pradesh, India,." 2004.

cxviii Human Rights Watch, Future Forsaken, 2004.

cxix Kaiser Family Foundation, HIV/AIDS in India – Policy Fact Sheet, Sept. 2006.

cxx Medical News Today, "Indian Health Ministry Proposes Fivefold Increase In Funding For HIV/AIDS Programs," Jan. 24, 2007.http://www.medicalnewstoday.com/medicalnews.php?newsid=61349

cxxi The Times of India, "India launches National Paediatric HIV/AIDS Initiative" by Kounteya Sinha http://timesofindia.indiatimes.com/Clintons_gift_for_HIV_kids/articleshow/644743.cms.

cxxii The Hindu, "Training for Doctors in Primary AIDS Care," March 18, 2007

http://www.hindu.com/2007/03/18/stories/2007031819370300.htm.

cxxiii The Hindu, "Nutritional Scheme for HIV Affected," March 18, 2007.

cxxiv Agence France-Press, "New HIV infections plunge by a third in southern India," http://www.aegis.com/NEWS/AFP/2006/AF060367.html.

cxxv Infochange India, http://www.infochangeindia.org/analysis131.jsp.

cxxvi ZeeNews.com, http://zeenews.com/articles.asp?rep=2&aid=365384&sid=NAT.

cxxvii Anjali Gopalan, Naz Foundation, Telephone Interview, April 22, 2007.

cxxviii Human Rights Watch, "AIDS in India: Money won't Solve Crisis, Rising Violence Against AIDS-affected People," November 13, 2002.

cxxix United States Agency for International Development, "Helping Indian Children with AIDS," June 22, 2006.

cxxx Bill Gates speech, Fifty-eighth World Health Assembly, May 16, 2005.

cxxxi The American Journal of Bio-Ethics, Light, "Will Lower Drug Prices Jeopardize Drug Research?" by Donald and Joel Lexchin, January 2004.

cxxxii United Nations "Notes for Press Briefing," January 8, 2003.

"Being unwanted, unloved, uncared for, forgotten by everybody, I think that is a much greater hunger, a much greater poverty than the person who has nothing to eat."

–*Mother Teresa*

.

The Price of a Child

The toddler running up to me was like a force of nature. Her short, chubby legs pumped underneath the ruffles of a frilly pink and green dress and her hands clapped furiously. A huge, wide-mouthed grin stole her face as she jumped around me, and in the space of that smile I could see the pure joy she felt at being alive.

I was amazed, because I recognized this little girl. Her deep, intense eyes were unmistakable. It was Sumitra, the child who had arrived at the Rourkela home one short year ago in the middle of the night, a starving nine-month-old who could not even cry.

"She's not only playing, she's being naughty," said Caroline with a smile. "I love it, because a child needs to be healthy to be naughty!"

I had just arrived at Manjeet's home for children, after spending the previous week immersed in the AIDS crisis in

Tamil Nadu and Andhra Pradesh. What a happy feeling it was to have Sumitra and a dozen other children pour over me in excited greetings, and to meet up with Caroline and Manjeet and other friends from the Miracle Foundation. After traveling throughout India over the month, it was a homecoming.

After arriving on an overnight train from Calcutta, I had made my way to the modest but charming hotel Caroline had reserved and collapsed into sleep for several hours. Later that afternoon our group climbed into Manjeet's SUV and drove through the town of Rourkela, then passing out of town drove for about half an hour through smaller villages. The driver talked and sent text messages on his mobile phone the whole way, his other hand pounding the horn as he swerved at high speeds around the huge, garishly decorated Tata trucks and the cows, aiming instead head-on toward every oncoming rickshaw and motorcycles carrying families of five. With sixty thousand traffic fatalities a year, India has only two percent of the world's roads but accounts for seven percent of its accidents. I had no trouble believing this.

Pulling into the gates of the ashram, I saw an expanse of dusty yard covered sporadically with grass and filled with playground equipment. Set a hundred yards back was the main house, a long and low building with a big front porch. This was where the babies and housemothers lived. Behind this front house was another expanse of yard, the cooking pit and the kitchen; then two other small buildings. One was the dormitory for the older children, and the other

was a computer lab set up with donations from Advanced
Micro Devices, Inc.

Half of the children here were Sumitra's age or younger
– under two years old. Because the home took in so many
unwed mothers there were many infants. The remaining
children were between three and ten years old.
Housemothers Joyti and Susan led me through the two
nursery rooms and showed me the babies. Many were
sleeping in their old-fashioned white swing cradles; others
sat in the cribs and stared at me as I walked by, or stretched
their arms out to be held. I picked up a solid boy named
Christ, while carefully dodging the occasional child
crawling on the mat-covered floor beneath us.

When I entered the toddler room, it was a different
scene altogether. Unlike Sumitra, who had happily run right
to me, the other children aged two or three were terrified of
me. The second they saw me they began to wail. Several
tried to run away so fast that their newly learned walking
skills failed them and they fell over with a thump, causing
them to cry even harder. Within seconds, each had made his
or her way to a housemother to whom they clung for dear
life, burying tiny faces to rid themselves of the sight of me.

I was taken aback at this reception. Accustomed to
children thronging me and rushing to sit in my lap or play
with me, my feelings were a bit hurt at this reaction of fear.
Caroline only laughed.

"It's good!" she reassured me. "It means they are so
bonded to their house mothers that they're fearful of
strangers. One of the biggest issues with children in

orphanages or institutional homes is their lack of attachment. Our kids have no problems with that!"

"Good point," I conceded, and tried not to take it personally. I moved on, across the back yard to the computer lab where a dozen elementary-school children sat before monitors, clicking away. Some were engrossed in educational games involving counting or English words; others were writing short stories about themselves and their lives, overseen by a tutor.

The computer learning lab had been set up a year before with a grant from AMD's 50 x 15 initiative. This program aimed to enable affordable, accessible Internet connectivity and computing capabilities for fifty percent of the world's population by the year 2015. The particular focus was to eliminate the digital divide between industrialized and developing countries. The grant had provided ten computers and monitors and a server, and the tutor and housemothers used the lab to teach the children word processing and how to use a mouse and keyboard. Each child was busy with a project and flashed me a quick smile as I came by, before returning quickly to their screens.

The AMD website included a story about the Miracle Foundation learning lab, stating in part:

In a remote town in eastern India, AMD is helping provide computer access to some of its youngest inhabitants as part of its 50x15 initiative. Finding their way to the orphanage through various avenues, the children face a life of uncertainty. What's more, Birmitrapur is remote – 45 minutes by car from the nearest town of Rourkela – and faces significant challenges in infrastructure, power management, and connectivity. In the Learning Lab, the fundamental goal is to provide the children of the orphanage with educational capabilities and a means of keeping in touch with their adoptive parents around the world. Through the opening of the Learning Lab, a new world has been opened to these children, most of whom have never seen a computer; much less had the opportunity to use one. Not only do these children acquire life skills at the orphanage, but now they learn about technology-driven opportunities and discover a new way of learning about the world.

* * *

In the older kids' dormitory next door, I peeked in on boys and girls who were doing minor chores such as picking up their sleeping areas, or were bent over their school notebooks in study. I met a boy named Amir, a seven year old with funny little ears that stuck straight out from the sides of his head and an easy smile that turned down at the corners. He wore a sporty blue and orange shirt over a pair of shorts. He was very friendly and I could tell he wanted to talk, but seemed a little shy about it. I wasn't sure if it was because I was a stranger or he was struggling with English, a new language for him.

"Hi, Amir, it's very nice to meet you." I sat down with him and house mother Joyti to get to know him, Joyti translating my questions. What was his favorite color, his favorite food, who were his best friends at the home? He answered me easily as he continued to smile and his eyes darted this way and that, Joyti repeating what he said in English.

"What do you want to be when you grow up?" I asked. Like with all children, there were some pretty standard answers I usually was given in response to this question. Teacher or police officer were the most commonly identified goals, although I also heard dancer, lawyer and social worker quite often.

Amir grew serious, and contemplated my question for some time. I could see him rolling it over in his mind, all the possibilities as he truly gave thought to what he'd most like to be. Then his eyes lit up and he smiled his biggest grin yet, and announced his response in Hindi.

Joyti turned to me. "He says he wants to be a father when he grows up."

The answer hit me square in the chest. I looked at Amir, his sparkling eyes following the other kids around the play yard. This small boy who had no father, and yet his dreams were to *be* a father. Perhaps to know that connection and joy of family. Perhaps to love his own child and be the kind of real father that he had never known. Whatever the reasons, it was clear that Amir felt the gaping hole of what was absent in his world. He glanced up at me again before racing off across the red dirt to join his friends.

* * *

At night the volunteers gathered for dinner and to exchange our stories, thoughts and experiences with the children. Besides Caroline and myself, our group included a Miracle Foundation staff member, several newcomers to India and Kathleen, who had been on that first trip I had taken two years previously.

India was in the semi-finals of the Cricket World Cup at that time, and all the restaurant workers were wearing Team India jerseys and keeping one eye on the television in the corner, where their country was squaring off with Sri Lanka. Over steaming platters of rice and biryana, ginger shrimp and fish tikka, we chatted about our days at Manjeet's home.

To my relief, I wasn't the only one the toddlers were terrified of. "Am I that scary?" Kathleen asked. But the older children, she added, were only too happy to play with her. "They call me Auntie and ask me all kinds of questions constantly – where I live, my age, and would I come back again."

Danny, on his first visit to India, said, "I expected the orphanage to be totally sad and depressing, but they are the coolest bunch of small people I've ever seen, all running around with smiles on their faces." He talked about one boy, Bijay, who had taken a particular liking to Danny and followed him everywhere.

"Whenever I sat down he was the first one in my lap and he would just start talking and smiling. Fifteen minutes later there are twelve kids crawling all over me, and he is still talking and smiling. I still have no idea what he was talking about but that didn't matter in the least,"

Danny said. "I could have told him goats were eating his shorts; he didn't care."

Another volunteer, Rebecca, and Raime, the Miracle Foundation employee, regaled us with hilarious tales of their shopping adventures. Having been given a donation by Danny to purchase various items for the kids and their upkeep, they took off for the market with Manjeet's wife, Pumi. "First we were buying kitchen supplies, so we had to go to the spoon store for spoons, then we had to go to the pot store for pots," Rebecca told us. "The funny thing is, we passed four or five different vendor stalls selling spoons or pots, and I would say 'There's spoons!' But Pumi would insist, 'No those aren't the good spoons.' And so we would keep going." She shook her head, laughing.

"When we bought uniforms for the kids, they needed to be green. I bet we went to six different shops before we found the 'right' shade of material," she continued. "At one point Pumi held two different fabric swatches out to me and asked which green I thought was better. But they both looked exactly the same to me!"

Kathleen and I caught each other's eye across the table and chuckled, recalling our own eventful Indian shopping expedition. For his part, Danny was amazed and impressed with what his two hundred U.S. dollars had bought: sixty pairs of shoes and forty baby outfits, as well as soccer balls and other assorted sporting goods.

Continuing the shopping saga, Raime added, "And then they brought the foot juice."

"The *foot* juice?" I questioned, not sure if I'd heard right.

"Well, it was actually sugar cane juice, which sounds really good, right? But unfortunately, it smelled just like feet!"

The knot of restaurant staff in their blue and orange jerseys grinned to each other at *our* uncontrolled laughter; even though they had no idea what was so funny, we were definitely a source of amusement.

* * *

The next day, the toddlers were just as afraid of us as ever and ran screeching to the housemothers as soon as they spotted one of us. We gave them their space, playing with the older children on the playground equipment or card games on the long front porch. I spent a good part of the afternoon in the baby room with Joyti and Susan, watching them feed the small children. They each sat on a mat on the floor with five or six older infants in a circle around them, perched on their diapered rumps precariously. Occasionally one made too sudden a movement and toppled over, or another would crawl a few feet away in distraction. But mostly, they sat looking up at either Joyti or Susan, focused intently on the bowls of cereal they held and fed by the spoonful to each child in turn. They looked like baby birds in the nest, faces upturned expectantly for mama bird to drop a goody into their waiting mouths.

When mealtime was done and bits of cereal cleaned from faces, fingers, necks, ears and even toes, I picked up

Jusab and went out to the porch. Sitting quietly with the ten month old falling asleep on my lap with a full belly, Susan slid into the chair beside me.

"Is this your first time in India?" she asked shyly.

"No, it's my third visit actually," I said. "But, it's my first time to Rourkela." I told her about the previous three weeks and all the places I'd been before arriving there.

"Do you know any Hindi?" she wanted to know.

"I only know a few words, but I have thought about learning. I guess I should, since I've been spending so much time here. And I have friends at home I could practice with."

She assured me that it was a very easy language to pick up. We talked about temples, Indian food and yoga. Susan was delighted to find out I was an avid practitioner and had been for years. "I do my yoga every morning at dawn," she said.

"I wish I could say I was that dedicated," I laughed. Truthfully, I was amazed that she remained committed to her practice and to taking that time for herself to start her day. Susan and all the housemothers worked constantly, typically in charge of three babies each, and always had a child or two in their arms. They ate with them, cared for them, even slept with them. I never saw the housemothers take a break while I was there; these babies where quite literally their entire lives, this place their home. I both admired them and felt grateful to them.

Just then a stray soccer ball careened up onto the porch, from the group of boys playing in the yard. Manjeet, standing nearby, picked it up and grinned before kicking it hard back out to them. He glanced back at me. "I used to be a soccer player in college," he said before trotting out to join the game. It seemed that every time I saw Manjeet, I learned some new and interesting tidbit about him that I never would have suspected. I sat on the porch and watched as he wove in between boys half his size, moving the ball down the field and passing it to other players, teaching them moves, yelling and laughing as if he, too, were ten years old.

* * *

Because there were so many infants in the Rourkela home, our time there consisted of a lot of holding babies and rocking. The next afternoon I was sitting by myself on the front porch, cradling eight-month-old Luane who was fast asleep and drooling on my arm, when Manjeet walked out. I had been reminding him all week that I wanted to talk to him at some point to ask more in-depth questions about his work and any new developments.

"Shelley!" he exclaimed when he spied me.

"Yes, sir?" I responded playfully.

"My interview with you is free of charge!" He held a straight face for a moment before cracking a smile. I laughed at his dry humor and he sat down next to me, gazing at the sleeping child on my lap. The turban he wore that day was bright red, and sweat stained his beige polo-style shirt. He looked tired.

"Next year, these babies will be gone," he said. "They will be adopted domestically, by Indian families. But there will be fifty more."

"The adoption program is going well, then?"

"We are not doing adoptions at the moment," Manjeet replied, to my surprise. I had not known this, and asked what happened. "The government revoked all adoption agency licenses a couple of months ago, and we had to reapply."

"Why did they do that?"

"It was due to some problem adoptions, so they stopped all of them. Adoption is a very sensitive and controversial issue. Protecting children from exploitation is paramount. There are many unethical and abusive organizations involved in the 'business' of adoption." He went on to explain that Pumi had recently gone to Cuttack to meet with Orissa state ministers for the new license. "We foresee being able to resume adoptions by October," Manjeet said.

In Andhra Pradesh to the south, just days before I had arrived at Manjeet's, I had read two different newspaper articles about people trying to sell babies right on the street. The *Calcutta Telegraph* ran the story of a woman who had her three-day-old daughter up for sale at a bus station. She was asking for bus fare in exchange for her daughter – seventy rupees, less than two U.S. dollars – who lay on a cloth at her feet. Her husband had left her after the baby's sex had been determined by a pre-natal test; it was their sixth girl, and the woman told police that she wanted to give away her other five daughters as well.

The newspaper article described a similar, but widespread, scheme in the woman's tribal hamlet a decade before, which had involved the illegal adoptions of hundreds of female children. According to tribal welfare minister Redya Nayak, the village was known to "get rid of the babies in various ways," either through selling them or, if that was unsuccessful, simply starving them.[cxxxiii]

The second story also involved a woman from a village in the same area who had seven daughters and, like the first woman, wanted to sell her newborn girl.[cxxxiv] Both of these infants were taken to Sishu Vihar, a home run by the Women and Child Welfare Department. Unfortunately, many children who ended up in institutional care would still fall victim to unethical adoptions because of the large number of fraudulent orphanage and adoption organizations, and the lack of adequate regulations and government oversight. Both accredited and unauthorized placement agencies have been raided and accused of commercializing adoption.

Using scouts or brokers to identify children in these tribal hamlets, they prey on destitute and illiterate parents and falsify records in order to adopt the children out, making big profits. The well-respected magazine *India Today* ran an expose of this practice in 2001, illuminating hundreds of children who had been "rescued from institutions with a question mark, up in the shop window, their souls commodified, a profit margin marked against their existence."ᶜˣˣˣᵛ

In other cases, children were not bought from their parents but simply kidnapped. In May 2007 a four-year-old boy, Mohit, who had been reported missing was taken from a Delhi railway station to Delhi Council for Child Welfare. Unlike the image its name implies, the enterprise is actually a private adoption agency better known as Palna. When Mohit's frantic parents finally located him, officials at Palna were uncooperative and refused to let them take the boy home. The couple had to enlist the help of the local Child Welfare Committee, which the government has established around the country and which are vested with judicial powers. Finally, on these legal orders, the parents were reunited with their son.

The Indian Department of Social Welfare (DSW) reported that such agencies "are getting children through legal or illegal means and are selling them in the market. The foreigners give higher prices, therefore they prefer to sell them to the foreigners." Despite a long waiting list of hopeful adoptive parents, adoption agencies ignore poor prospective parents in favor of wealthy Indians and foreign nationals. A senior DSW official said that if Mohit's parents had not been so persistent and sought legal government help, their son would likely have languished at Palna for months while the agency secured an illegal relinquishment and then given the child to complete strangers – for a large profit, of course.ᶜˣˣˣᵛⁱ

Caroline had told me that, by her estimation and experience visiting and researching dozens of orphanages, some sort of fraud was present in sixty to seventy percent of orphanages and adoption agencies. I asked Manjeet if he agreed with that figure.

"Yes, yes, it is what we see. There is much corruption in India." He held up a hand with three fingers outstretched. "There are three main areas of corruption: siphoning off government money; bribes to officials – usually a ten percent kickback; and misappropriation." He ticked each of these off as he spoke. I knew that as a former government auditor, Manjeet was an expert on this subject. "The money is not being used for the stated purposes. Donors have no recourse but to stop their donations. There is no transparency, and auditing is very weak. There are some very good government leaders, but the problem is so huge, so imbedded…" He trailed off and sighed heavily. "It's hard to make change happen."

We sat in silence for a few moments. Manjeet seemed lost in his own thoughts, introspective and perhaps a little dejected. I didn't know what to say; I had never seen him like this. He was always upbeat and cheerful, extremely energetic and ready to tackle any problem. Caroline once commented that Manjeet got more done in a day than most people do in a month.

After a while he spoke again. "Also, most of the money is going to urban cities. Very little gets to the rural areas, which is where it is needed the most. There is a huge divide and the poor are growing in number, and getting poorer."

I wasn't sure about the validity of the overall numbers of poor growing larger. My own research had yielded many reports that showed how the country's recent economic growth had pushed more Indians out of poverty than ever before. However, as far as that growth not reaching the rural areas, and the divide between rural and urban – that seemed to be a consensus. The major cities of India had significant problems and masses of urban poor living in slums; a 2006 UN-Habitat world report found that people living in urban poverty were worse off than their rural counterparts.[cxxxvii] However, the numbers of people living in rural poverty are more than three and a half times greater than those living in urban poverty, making up seventy-seven percent of the total poor in India.[cxxxviii]

Manjeet believed that much of the violence in the country – once rare but now a growing problem – was caused by inequities of both wealth and caste. "Abject poverty makes people desperate, hopeless. They have nothing left to lose. They feel, I am going to die anyway, of hunger and poverty. So why not die this way, fighting at least."

He grew more despondent as he talked. "India is the world's largest democracy, but it is a failure. My country is failing." He made his little tsk-tsk clicking noise against his teeth and shook his head sadly, eyes tearing up behind his glasses. "I am very emotional about this. Sometimes I, too, feel very hopeless. I think the problem is too big. What can be done? What difference am I really making?"

I felt his gloom settling in me and I wanted to reassure him, to tell him to look around at these children to see the difference he was making. I often felt the way he did. When tackling such huge and depressing problems it was easy to become pessimistic. Yet, there were always rays of hope that pierced through those clouds of negativity – success stories, individual lives changed, rather than focusing on the overall problems. Inspiring people who made you feel that anything was possible. Mother Theresa once said, "If you can't feed a hundred people, then feed just one."

Everything of real importance in human history had been accomplished by people facing nearly insurmountable odds. If it were easy, everyone would be doing it; if it were easy, it would not need so desperately to be done. Surely Dr. Martin Luther King, Jr., Mahatma Gandhi and Nelson Mandela had felt discouraged in countless moments; but their world-changing legacies came about because they refused to give up. Manjeet was one of those inspiring people to me; and although I knew that he, like anyone, would surely be overcome by the task at times, to see him lose heart truly shook me.

---

cxxxiii Calcutta Telegraph, "Baby on Sale for Bus Fare," March 21, 2007.

cxxxiv Hyderabad Chronicle, "Woman Tries to Sell Baby, Grilled," March 19, 2007.

cxxxv India Today, "Children on Sale" by Amarnath K. Menon, May 7, 2001.

cxxxvi Tehelka, "Missing Children: The Business of Adoption" by Sanjay Dubey, July 7, 2007.

cxxxvii UN-Habitat, "Urban poor worse off than rural poor but good policies can reduce slums" by Lisa Schlein and Sven Krüger, June 18, 2006.

cxxxviii Economy Watch, "India Poverty," accessed November 18, 2007. http://www.economywatch.com/indianeconomy/poverty-in-india.html

"Be the change that you want to see in the world."

–Mahatma Gandhi

In Plain Sight but Invisible

Sitting on my backpack in the railway station two days later, I waited with Caroline and our group of three other volunteers for the train that would take us from Rourkela, where we had spent the week, to Papa's home in Cuttack. Waiting for me there were Santosh, Daina and the dozens of other children I had met my first day in India, more than two years before. I was jittery with the anticipation of seeing them again – the highlight of the month I had spent here.

Although it was a small-town station with only two platforms, the place was crowded and buzzing with activity at ten-thirty pm. Families sat together on benches and groups of young adults jostled each other loudly, while others lay prone and unaware against the walls, sleeping on the concrete. Porters who must have weighed less than me threw two or three pieces of heavy luggage on their heads, weaving through the crowds behind their clients. A woman held her naked baby out over the train tracks while it urinated.

Small kiosks sold food – Indian snacks such as fried dosas and chai tea as well as potato chips, sodas and candy bars – while other unofficial vendors set up pans right along the platform to fry samosas and vegetables to fill the pastry. Men walked up and down with their trays, calling a monotonous litany: "Chai! Chai-coffee! Coffee-chai!" The smell of curry and frying ghee butter mixed with human sweat and urine hung heavily above the rails. Although the ceilings were high, the air felt compressed and stuffy around me. The sound of hundreds of voices in several languages filled my ears – Hindi, Oriyan, Bengali. The only thing I didn't hear was English.

We hovered around our amassed baggage, far more than the five of us needed because many of the suitcases contained art supplies, games, small toys and treats for the children at Papa's orphanage, an overnight train ride away. Barbara, a volunteer, and Raime, the Miracle Foundation staff member from Austin, walked my way from a vendor shop holding snacks and sodas amid stares both covert and blatant from those they passed. We were the only white faces there.

Seemingly from nowhere, two boys appeared beside us. They looked about seven or eight years old and were alone. Silently they held out their hands, then brought them to their mouths, then extended them again in the universal language of begging. My eyes met Caroline's and she gave a small, sad shake of her head.

When face to face with such children – a common occurrence virtually everywhere in India – it felt impossible to ignore them, to say no. A struggle invariably began inside my soul and no matter how many times the situation happened, that struggle never lessened and was never resolved. The truth of the matter was that giving money to these children would not have any significant impact on their lives beyond a few moments. It might even worsen their circumstances; many of them turned money and food directly over to parents or other adults who were either exploiting them or simply trying to stay a step above starvation. Reinforcing the tactic of child beggars as a successful strategy merely continued the cycle. Activists and NGO workers almost unanimously advised that to *really* make a lasting impact for children like this, or in fact anyone in desperate need, one should support legitimate holistic programs that address root issues and long-term solutions.

In my head, I knew this was true. I donated many dollars and hours every year to non-profit organizations that work with vulnerable children, both in India and the United States. It was the reason I was here in the first place, volunteering in the orphanages. It was the reason I was writing this book. But in my heart, it was another story every time I was approached, every time children like these boys looked up at me with their haunted or, even worse, vacant eyes. It was so hard to wave them off, or look away and pretend not to see them. They always stayed with me long after they were gone and I was left wondering how they ended up there, what their lives were like, and where they would go next.

Our driver, Manish, yelled something at the two boys and slapped one of them on the head, admonishing them to leave us alone. Caroline cried out at the severe rebuke. The boys moved a few feet away and stopped soliciting; but their eyes remained fixed on us, silently beseeching. I searched their faces, perhaps looking for clues about their lives. I was acutely aware of the mountain of belongings surrounding the five of us, the suitcases containing toys and treats for other children, the plastic bags of food and drinks at our feet.

A horn blared the alert for our train's approach to the station. As we gathered our things for boarding, Caroline leaned in close to Raime and me. "You can leave a few things for them if you want," she whispered. "Just don't give it directly to them. Leave it behind." This was coming from the woman who had constantly lectured the teams all three times I had been on her volunteer trips not to give to any beggars, ever, for all the reasons just described. I looked at her and realized that, after years of this work and countless trips here, every time one of these children approached her the same struggle must also go on inside her.

I grabbed my backpack and a team suitcase as Raime readied her luggage. Just before we started down the platform to the boarding area, she and I pulled several candy bars and two bottles of soda from a plastic bag and set them on the ground. We stepped a few feet away and I looked toward the boys. They had not moved or taken their eyes off us. Amazingly, they didn't grab the snacks and run. They just stood there, staring at us. I looked at the candy, then back to the boys, and nodded my head. Hesitantly, the older one questioned me with his eyes and glanced at the pile on the floor for the first time. I nodded again. Raime and I moved a little farther away and like a shot, the boys quickly snatched up what we'd left and darted off at a blazing run.

After we climbed on the train and found our seats, I stowed my backpack under a side bench and sat down. Within moments, there was a knock on the window. I looked out and the two boys were standing on the platform, now with several other boys. They were all grinning from ear to ear. "One more, auntie!" they shouted. I smiled and waved at them, but the train was already pulling out of the station. As paltry as it seemed, I was glad we left the candy and hoped it made them happy even if it was only for a moment. I wondered what their names were, and what would happen to them tomorrow.

* * *

There are thousands upon thousands of such children in India; waves of people step over and around them every day without ever really seeing them. As crowds of people disembark from the trains – commuters, businessmen, families, university students, mothers and babies, young trendy urbanites with their iPods – they leave the platforms and swarm to the exits. But some remain behind – the small and permanent residents, the ones for whom the railway station is their only home. Of all the vulnerable children they are the least hidden, in plain sight right on the platforms or outside on the pavement, yet they are perhaps the most invisible of all.

Their numbers as quoted by various agencies are so wide they are almost meaningless. One 1994 report by UNICEF estimated eleven million street children in India; the United Nations High Commissioner for Human Rights stated eighteen million.[cxxxix] Some NGOs put the figure as high as a hundred million.[cxl] Accurate statistics are hard to pin down because the children's lives are never constant and their mobility is as much as seventy percent.[cxli] Many of them live right on the sidewalks or in slums of extreme deprivation. Although I don't know the specific circumstances of the boys in the Rourkela station that March, uncounted numbers of children live in railway stations all over the country.

Kids of all ages make their homes in these stations, often begging or picking through trash for a living. With the second largest rail network in the world carrying eleven million passengers each day, India's train stations play a major role in street children's lives.[cxlii] Many of those who run away take a train, often without even knowing where it is headed, and usually remain in the stations where they arrive because of access to toilet facilities and the ability to scratch out a meager existence from industry that springs up around rail travel: as luggage porters, shoe shiners, food or tea servers, rag pickers or beggars. They sleep under bridges, on the footpaths or on the platforms, sometimes mere feet from where the trains race by. They are at high risk for mistreatment, malnutrition, health problems and substance abuse. Glue sniffing is the most common drug problem for many of these children, who often yearn for an escape from the brutality of their lives.

With no supervision of any kind and largely unprotected by adults, they are extremely vulnerable to exploitation and violence, especially within the first days and weeks of leaving home.[cxliii] On average, a child arriving alone at a railway station will be approached by a predator, maybe a factory representative seeking cheap child labor or a brothel owner, within twenty minutes.[cxliv] Employers of kids who perform jobs such as rag and bottle collecting keep the children indebted to them. These victimizers know where to find children who won't be missed.

Seen as delinquents rather than victims of poverty, abusive families or an inadequate safety net, these children are constantly subjected to harassment by railway authorities and police, including forced monetary bribes to stay in the stations. A 2006 study found such mistreatment to be widespread. Eighty-five percent of street children reported abuse by police in the form of illegal detention and physical beatings; almost as many, more than eighty-one percent, said they had no one to go to for protection from such abuse.[cxlv] Some organizations, including Human Rights Watch, characterize physical abuse by police as torture instead of violence because of the position of power they hold over children, both as adults and law enforcement officers.

* * *

The dark side of Mumbai reveals an estimated 2.3 million who live either on the streets or in the slums.[cxlvi] Many of them are children, often on their own. Approximately thirty unaccompanied children arrive at the city's hundred and twenty-five train stations every day.[cxlvii]

I met some of these kids myself one sunny morning, three weeks before my encounter with the boys in the Rourkela station. Gyan, a social worker with the NGO Oasis India, escorted me to their Ashadeep program for street children at the Kurla train station. We took a taxi to the massive Victoria terminal, an historic station built in 1888 and named a World Heritage Site by UNESCO. The Gothic building looked more like a huge cathedral than a train station to me. I believed what I'd heard about it being one of the busiest stations in India as soon as we walked through the doors, where it seemed half of Mumbai had just gotten down from the trains and were coming straight at us. For ten minutes we fought our way against an endless flow of humanity until we reached the platforms.

I stood and literally gaped in amazement. The largest train station I had ever been in was Paddington in London, and I thought it was big. At Victoria, tracks and platforms stretched away in the cavernous building as far as I could see. Digital displays announcing arrivals and departures were overhead next to jumbotron monitors that played music videos and commercials extolling the virtues of various mobile phones and insurance plans. We stood waiting for our train, one of many suburban lines that radiated from this hub, while businessmen around us read newspapers and had their shoes shined.

From Victoria we traveled about twenty minutes to the Kurla station. Setting his backpack between his feet, Gyan told me a little about himself as we rode. Originally from Nepal, he had been an outreach social worker with Oasis India for four years. His focus was entirely street kids. Gyan's easy smile and quiet, polite manner seemed well suited to what I imagined was difficult and often distressing work.

When we exited the platform at Kurla, he led the way through an entire community that had sprung up around the station. I would never have known it existed, but around the train tracks and platforms there were lanes and homes and shop stalls, people cooking and washing their clothes and their babies, everyday life happening in this dusty railway village.

After winding through a maze that I would never find my way back out of alone, Gyan knocked at a locked door and another Ashadeep worker let us in. The tiny room was filled with nine boys, ranging in age from about eight to fourteen, playing games on the tile floor with two other male staff members while they took turns washing in the single bathroom. As they came out of the washroom, their hair was wet and combed neatly to one side. Their faces and hands were dusted with the talcum powder they patted on after washing to keep cool in the heat.

These boys all lived in the train station by night. Most were not from Mumbai, but were runaways from towns and villages as much as two or three days journey away, lured by dreams of making it big in Mumbai. The home of Bollywood movies, the city is the capital of India's dreams, where young people came chasing stardom and instant happiness. It was a familiar story in America, where runaways who flee to Hollywood or New York for the same reasons often are preyed upon instead.

Gyan and the other Oasis social workers spent much of each work day doing outreach in the train stations, searching for new children and befriending them in a non-threatening manner. They first simply gave the kids food and told them about the Ashadeep program, which means "lamp of hope." When the children came to Ashadeep they were offered a bath, secondhand clothing and the chance to regularly participate in activities such as games, movies and sports as well as medical check-ups. The caseworkers tried to protect them as much as possible from the dangers of the station.

"These boys lose their right to a childhood, education, and family," Gyan said as we watched the boys play. "They even lose their humanity."

The program also provided learning activities. Soon after my arrival, the games were put away and a math lesson began. The boys grew serious as they carefully wrote down numbers and did their sums. The interesting

foreigner in their midst was quickly forgotten and they
concentrated on their assignment, soaking up the learning
like a sponge and eager to show off their skills. I watched
these eight, ten and twelve year olds, who should be in
school every day, and thought about all the children who
take their education for granted. It was such a simple right
that it *should* be taken for granted as a right for all children.
This was the only schooling these boys had, and it made me
very fearful for their futures.

I noticed one of the boys struggling to write his math
problems. His arms were missing below the elbows and he
leaned over his notebook on the floor, holding a pencil in
his teeth and guiding it with the stub of his left arm.
Threads hung from where the sleeves had been cut off the
heavily stained shirt. His brown knees were scabby below
his shorts; I could see only the top of his head, short black
hairs bristling from his scalp, as he bent over his work
laboriously.

His name was Mohammed Rashid. About twelve years
old, he was one of the rare local children, a Muslim boy
with family nearby. He lived at the Kurla station with the
other boys part of the time, and sometimes with his family.
When he was four or five, Rashid suffered some sort of
injury to both his hands – exactly what Gyan either didn't
know or wouldn't tell me. Such vagueness seemed common
for such children who often didn't know their birthdays or
exactly how old they were. An infection set into Rashid's
hands and spread. The desperately poor family lacked the

money for a proper operation and medical treatment, so both of his arms were amputated above the elbows.

Rashid voraciously ate up anything and everything taught to him. "He loves to learn. He is an extremely smart boy," said Gyan. "Unfortunately, his parents use his disability to solicit alms, making him beg on the streets or in the station." Rashid would be a perfect candidate for boarding school, if his family could be persuaded to give permission for him to go. Oasis India could arrange a place for the boy, but Gyan felt it was unlikely to happen. "It would mean a loss of income from his begging for the family."

Rashid looked up at me and posed proudly for a photo, tilting his head to face the camera at an angle over his shoulder. His slanting eyes crinkled at the outside corners above his broad nose as he gave me the barest of smiles.

Once a boy had been coming to Ashadeep regularly and wanted to leave the railway life, Gyan or another caseworker would contact any family members to work on a possible reunification and get the child into school. They went to the home to assess safety for the child's return and also arranged a visit by the police. Gyan and the other social workers educated parents about caring for their children and offered them resources. If a boy was placed back with his family, follow-up visits continued.

Gyan said most such reunifications were successful. The few boys who returned to Ashadeep usually did so for job training as they grew older. From the sixty boys helped last year, ten to fifteen remained at Kurla. The others were either placed back with their families or in residential homes and schools, or they simply left the station.

Because many of them fled abusive homes or were forced to leave, going back to family was not always an option. In those cases, he tried to get the boys into group residential homes, boarding schools, or rehabilitation centers. Some had been so abused and were so frightened of their parents, they did not want to go back to secure the necessary permission, not even with an Ashadeep representative at their side.

"I tell the boys that as long as we are with them, no one can raise hands against them any longer," Gyan said. "But still, they are sometimes too afraid."

He showed me reports on other children, filled out each time a caseworker made contact. One such report on a boy named Samir gave me a glimpse into what the kids' daily lives were like outside these walls. First contacted at the Kurla station in November 2006, Samir was a seventeen-year-old Muslim boy who came to Mumbai from an outlying town when he ran away from home. Samir told the Oasis staff worker that he was physically abused and beaten at home and that his father threw him out. He had not been in contact with his family since leaving. His most immediate need was for clothing. He had been staying at Kurla for fifteen days at the time contact was made and was sustaining himself through rag picking, earning fifty to one hundred rupees a day ($1.00-2.50 USD) by selling the cast-off trash he collected to recyclers. He spent his money on food, movies, tea and paan – leaves filled with betel nuts, spices or tobacco. Movies were his favorite past-time.

Samir also reported picking up a cigarette habit from other railway boys who had become his friends. When asked if he had any knowledge about HIV/AIDS, Samir answered no. The living conditions and lack of nutrition make street children vulnerable to many health problems, with a particularly high risk for HIV. A recent survey among a hundred street children at a Delhi railway station revealed that eighty-six percent of boys in the fourteen to eighteen year old age group were sexually active; however an abysmally low number of them knew about safe sex protection. Not one of them reported having ever used a condom.[cxlviii] Across the country in the state of Andhra Pradesh, sexual activity among street children was found to be high, with a close association between street children and sex workers. Exposure to sexually transmitted diseases was common, with gonorrhea present among forty-four percent of street children.[cxlix]

Samir did not want to go back home. He didn't believe that his parents cared about him, and he liked the freedom of the street life. He had completed the fifth grade level in school; most boys his age were at the tenth level. When asked if he would like to study further Samir said he would, particularly to study Urdu language. He said that the best way Ashadeep could help him, however, was by assisting him to secure work. His dream was to become a police officer.

For most of these boys, such aspirations would remain only that. The longer they were on the street, the more distant those dreams became. Their hopes and their Bollywood fantasies were wispy and tenuous, and could easily dissipate into thin air until there was nothing left of them. But in the safety of the Ashadeep center, at least, those small dreams were protected and given some possibilities. When they left this room they returned to the hard truth of the actual, where such imaginings must seem a useless frivolity. Sleeping in the railway station, they were back in the world – not one they could make with their dreams, but the one that had made them.

I asked Gyan a question that had been in my mind since walking into the center. "Why are there only boys in the program?"

"The majority of kids living in the train stations are boys," he replied. "We see maybe ten percent girls." He attributed this to two reasons. First, boys were more likely than girls to run away from home and leave their villages. Second, for the females who did arrive at the train stations, they were the first to disappear. The sex trade swallowed them up immediately. Every hour four new girls and women enter prostitution – three of them against their will.[cl] An estimated fifteen percent of the 2.3 million prostitutes in India are children under fifteen,[cli] and over forty percent of sex workers become involved in such work before they are eighteen.[clii] One of the biggest challenges is reaching these girls before their exploiters do.

Some years ago, nine-year-old Shaila came to the

Ashadeep center with her sisters and friends from the street. They were aggressive, badly behaved and addicted to sniffing solvents and chewing tobacco. Seeming to have no further need for childhood, Shaila set about disposing of it. She began working in the sex trade as a means for survival and at fifteen had her first child. Due to extreme weakness and malnutrition, the child did not live. Two years later, Shaila gave birth again. This baby was born without an anal opening and required immediate surgery for survival.

Oasis India helped with raising money for the operation. After release from the hospital, Shaila and her baby were placed at the Purnata Bhavan residential home and rehabilitation center, which provided health care, childcare and vocational training in a family environment. Shaila, however, did not want to be confined to the home and within a day had run away from Purnata Bhavan with her baby. Two weeks later, Oasis staff found her back at the railway station.

"Many of these girls remain on the streets," Oasis Communications Manager Divya Kottadiel told me later that day. "Once they've been in the sex trade very long, no matter how abusive, it becomes more difficult to get them out of it."

For years Shaila resisted the love, care, concern and aid offered by the Oasis staff members. Today, she continues to resist. She prefers to live on her own on the crowded, dirty railway platform than in a safe, clean environment. When Ashadeep caseworkers occasionally identify girls such as Shaila in the stations, they refer them to other NGOs that have programs for street girls, such as Purnata Bhavan and another railway operation, Salaam Baalak Trust.

* * *

Salaam Baalak Trust was born of a 1988 movie about just such street kids. *Salaam Bombay!* follows a young boy, Chaipau, who takes a train journey just like many of the boys at Kurla station and ends up wandering alone in Bombay (now Mumbai). He gets by selling chai for a tea stall and eventually makes friends with other children living in the streets, railway stations and brothels of the city. Alternately devastating and uplifting, *Salaam Bombay!* chronicles the day-to-day lives of Chaipau and his friends with emotional resonance, but a stark lack of moralistic judgment, illuminating the hardships such children face.

The movie was shot entirely on location on the streets of Bombay, and most of the young actors were not professionals but actual street children. Filmmaker Mira Nair was struck by the large presence of such children in Bombay and decided to make a film about their lives. Once the movie was completed, Nair felt the message should not stop there. With her mother, she started a nonprofit organization to rehabilitate and support the children featured in the film. The initial funding for Salaam Baalak Trust (SBT) came from revenues from the movie.

Nair's mother, Praveen, became the Managing Trustee and at seventy-six years old is still going strong with the SBT mission today. When Mrs. Nair was in New York for the premier of her daughter's newest movie, *The Namesake*, I spoke to her by telephone from my home in Austin. Echoing what Gyan had told me about the additional hardships faced by girls and their vulnerability to the sex trade, she confirmed, "The presence of a girl on the street is not as prominent as the boys." The options for adolescent and teenage girls left on their own are unspeakable.

Mrs. Nair told me a story that haunted her. Not long after SBT was started, a child of about twelve used to come to the shelter regularly for food, medical care and the games and learning activities. Then he suddenly disappeared. Despite their best search efforts no one on the SBT team could find him.

"And then we discovered that it was a girl who had been masquerading as a boy," said Mrs. Nair, "because for a girl to exist at the railway station was very difficult." As the child entered puberty, it became physically impossible to pass herself off as a boy. Sadly, Mrs. Nair never found the child or discovered what happened to her.

The organization started very small, with twenty to twenty-five children in Delhi and Mumbai. Mrs. Nair recalled how she and the first SBT outreach workers roamed the railway stations for six to eight weeks trying to reach out to the children, without success. "Initially it was very difficult because these kids do not trust easily due to their past experiences. At every stage they have been abused and exploited, by their families or the community. Even the police, social workers, government organizations – everywhere."

It took weeks to break the ice with children, and Mrs. Nair was frustrated by the slow progress. Then one boy became very sick. With nowhere else to turn, his friends called SBT. It was a turning point for these children who had been so let down in the past. Social workers took the boy to the hospital and cared for him through his illness, proving themselves to the railway children community.

"Now, our presence at the railway stations is very prominent. By word of mouth, the children come to us," Mrs. Nair relayed happily. This word of mouth is critical in early interventions with new children arriving in the stations or streets, as other kids tell them where to find a trusted adult along with shelter, food and other necessities.

Salaam Bombay! went on to receive worldwide acclaim, nominated for an Academy Award for best foreign film and garnering ten international awards including the Camera D'Or award at the Cannes Film Festival. Quite an incredible journey for these young people whose day-to-day lives we can barely begin to comprehend.

* * *

Coincidentally, Praveen Nair and her daughter Mira – the award-winning international filmmaker of movies such as *Vanity Fair* starring Reese Witherspoon and *Mississippi Masala* with Denzel Washington – are originally from Bhubaneswar, near Papa's orphanage in the state of Orissa. Mrs. Nair told me she would like to see more expansion to the rural areas and villages such as Papa's location. Eighty percent of the railway and street children who end up in big cities come from these outlying areas. If the children could be assisted in their home towns, before they arrive alone in Delhi, Calcutta or Mumbai, the effort to keep them off the streets would be more successful.

"By the time they reach the urban areas, the damage has already been done," Mrs. Nair said. Even so, SBT has initiated prevention programs within large cities. They offer their services not only to railway and other runaway or homeless children, but also to local children living in neighboring slums with their families. It's a proactive, community-based approach with several benefits. It prevents many children who live in the slums from ending up on the streets themselves, and helps reduce the stigma that street children endure from surrounding citizens – beliefs that such children are criminals or delinquents, or simple disdain at the sight of them.

"Most people dismiss the street children as a nuisance: vagabonds, petty thieves and dirty kids." But Mrs. Nair disagreed. "They are the smartest kids, very hard-working. If they are given the right environment – the nurturing that every kid deserves – they are as good as any other child. Their spirit of survival is their biggest strength. It is that spirit we want to develop in a more positive manner." Her pride in the children was evident in her voice; as well as her sense of accomplishment that SBT has been able to mainstream so many of those they've helped. Former street children from the SBT program have gone on to success in many professions, started families, and even bought their own homes.

* * *

In 2006, the Ahmedabad Study Action Group conducted an extensive research and interview process with street children. The purpose was to get a more accurate view of the lives of these children, the conditions and issues they face; as well as an assessment of their greatest needs in order to best plan for ways to successfully address them. Like Mrs. Nair, the study group concluded, "The general public does not seem to have a healthy attitude towards street children. Because of the petty occupations they take up for their survival and the conditions in which they live, they are often looked down upon by others. Their homelessness makes them unacceptable to others."

When street children themselves were directly questioned by the researchers, the most imperative need reported was for shelter. Shelters help protect children not only from the elements, but from the harassment they experience when they have to sleep on platforms and footpaths. Other needs, in order of priority given by the children, were clothing, medical treatment, and access to toilets and bathing facilities.[cliii] As I read the report, what struck me was the item missing from the children's own declaration of needs – food. One of the most imperative necessities in life was not even mentioned. In their daily struggle for mere survival it seemed to be viewed as a luxury, an afterthought, for these kids.

"If you can get to them within the first few days or weeks, you've got a much better chance of stopping them from becoming a long term street child," said John Nonhebel, Executive Director of Oasis India, in his office after my visit to the Kurla railway station. "Once that happens, it can be extremely difficult to reach them. They can become addicted to the streets, as well as solvents or alcohol. They get addicted to that life and a lot of times it's really hard to change."

John, who is originally from England, first came to Oasis India as a volunteer in the early 1990s. It's been said that outsiders have come to India throughout history to try to conquer it or change it, but a funny thing always happens – India takes these foreigners and makes them Indian. This is exactly what happened to John. As he related to me, he "just kept coming back" until he became an Oasis staff member and eventually Executive Director. In those early days, the aim of the organization was all about opportunity – where they saw a need, they jumped in.

"But, out of opportunity you start thinking about strategy, you start thinking about development issues. We've been involved with caring for the children on the railway platforms for a number of years, trying to reintegrate them with families or get them into school. But strategically, our mind is turning now to thinking about what we can do to really make a difference. What impact do we want to have?" John asked. "Let's try and increase our impact – not just touching the surface level issues."

He emphasized the need for proactive rather than reactive initiatives, for interventions to be put into place much earlier for children like the boys at the Kurla train station. Like Praveen Nair, he believed it was vital to focus on the issues that caused children to be on the streets in the first place – rural poverty, lack of opportunities and devaluation of education.

John called this approach the Early Encounter Strategy and explained that Oasis was moving in that direction, so that they could reach children before they became homeless or were exploited. In fact, the Ashadeep program was being re-evaluated at the time of my visit, to assess its impact in comparison to the greater need for prevention and earlier intervention.

After my experiences with railway children, my visit to the Kurla station and my research, the need to catch these children right away was obvious to me; once any child was plucked away from the station they were almost always lost. Yet I couldn't help but think of those boys I spent the day with – the face of Rashid, struggling with the pencil between his teeth and amputated arm, floated inside the backs of my eyes when I closed them. And I wondered, if the Ashadeep center closed, where would those children go now?

* * *

Sitting on the train in March 2007, after pulling out of the Rourkela depot where we encountered the boys asking us for something, anything, I was on my way back to Santosh and Daina again. Some of the kids living in the Miracle Foundation homes had been street children just like those boys, like the children Oasis and Salaam Baalak Trust come across every day, begging or ragpicking to sustain themselves. One of them was a teenage girl named Milli.

Tall, with thick eyebrows and a soft chin-length bob with bangs sweeping across her forehead, Milli was soft-spoken and helpful. She often had a smaller child on her hip or in her lap. When she smiled her eyes literally sparkled and her entire upper lip stretched wide to reveal full gums and straight, white upper teeth.

Milli had lived at Papa's orphanage for a long time. When she was just four years old, her stepfather grew tired of raising another man's child and sent her out. Too young even to be in school, she was found begging in the streets and brought to the children's home.

Some children like Milli are helped through a service called ChildLine. The person who found Milli already knew about Papa's home and took her there. Others who find such children – neighbors, teachers, social workers – may not know where to take them or who can help them. ChildLine was set up in 1998 in partnership between the government and numerous NGOs to provide a 24-hour emergency hotline for children in need of assistance; the Delhi ChildLine service is operated by Salaam Baalak Trust. In its ten years of existence, ChildLine has taken nearly ten million calls and helped almost three million children throughout India. In the last year, Papa had two new children placed in his home through ChildLine.

* * *

The children living in railway stations and on the streets need, often crave, a sense of concern and protection from adults. More than sixty percent of those questioned in the Ahmedabad study expressed a desire for more than just a roof over their heads, but for a real home. The safety provided by caring adults can help them reach a healthy adulthood full of opportunities for their futures. More than that, such structure and protection give them a sense of love and self-worth – things every child deserves. Street children acutely feel the absence of this, in the lack of a home.

"They should have at least that much," said Praveen Nair. "They need care and love. We don't refuse any child, but we don't force any child to come to us. These kids are very fond of their freedom."

It was a dichotomy I heard time and again, that street children resist the boundaries that would come with the security of the homes they dream about. They don't want to be told what to do, they rebel against rules and discipline set by parents or other authority figures – yet, it is this which they most need. "Many children on the streets continue to live on the streets, despite safer options," said Divya Kottadiel of Oasis. "The thought of being confined to four walls frightens them and they prefer to live in 'freedom' out on the streets."

But for these children, the price of freedom is very high. They pay with their childhood, their innocence, and sometimes their very lives.

cxxxix Infochange India, "Platform No. 6, New Delhi Station, is Home for These Children," September 2003. http://www.infochangeindia.org/storyofcprint.jsp?recordno=2457.

cxl Office of the United Nations High Commissioner for Human Rights, <u>COMMITTEE ON RIGHTS OF CHILD REVIEWS SECOND PERIODIC REPORT OF INDIA,</u> April 2004. - http://www.unhchr.ch/huricane/huricane.nsf/0/E6DB9B85AA3 A1304C1256E23003551D8?opendocument.

cxli Vasavya Mahila Mandali, "Burning Childhood: The Child on the Street."

cxlii Railway Children, Newsletter No. 11, Spring 2004.

cxliii Railway Children, Newsletter No. 11, Spring 2004.

cxliv Praveen Nair, personal interview, May 9, 2007.

cxlv Ahmedabad Study Action Group, <u>Children Without Childhood,</u> by Harish Joshi, Leela Visaria and Rajesh Bhat, 2006.

cxlvi India Together, "Who's Teaching Whom?" by Jemma Purdey, October 2004.

cxlvii The Christian Science Monitor: "India's Railway Children," by Andrew Strickler, August 4, 2004.

cxlviii Salaam Baalak Trust, Annual Report 2002-2003, http://www.salaambaalaktrust.com/statistics03.asp.

cxlix Vasavya Mahila Mandali, "Burning Childhood: The Child on the Street."

cl Railway Children, "Girls on the Streets."

cli The Global March Against Child Labor, "Report on the Worst Forms of Child Labour." June 1998.

clii UNICEF website, "The Picture in India," May 14, 2007. http://www.unicef.org/india/child_protection_152.htm.

cliii Ahmedabad Study Action Group, <u>Children Without Childhood,</u> by Harish Joshi, Leela Visaria and Rajesh Bhat, 2006.

"A lot of people are waiting for Martin Luther King or
Mahatma Gandhi to come back -- but they are gone. We are
it. It is up to us. It is up to you."

– Marian Wright Edelman

Hope Springs Eternal

When our group of five arrived from Rourkela at the train station in Cuttack at six a.m., Rohit was waiting to collect us. Rohit had been our driver during every trip, and he helped pile our things into the SUV and took us to the hotel a few kilometers away. We spent most of the morning resting; between the narrow, hard bunks jostling above the tracks as the train sped over them, the chai and newspaper merchants making their endless rounds, the constant station stops and accompanying announcements and the snoring of strangers in close quarters, overnight Indian trains are not the most conducive places for a good night's sleep.

A few hours later we headed to Papa's orphanage. It felt at once like it had been ages since I had seen them all and as if we had just been together yesterday. Pulling through the gates, the children were waiting for us and engulfed the vehicle as soon as it came to a halt. I gently opened my door against a pressing wave of little bodies and climbed out, hugging two and three kids at a time as all of us grinned our joy at the reunion. Sumi and Mami and Meena were among the first at my side, as boys like Tapas and Nirod extended their arms above the little girls' heads for a manly handshake.

I moved away from the car and started toward the courtyard, and more children came streaming from the direction of the dorms. Suddenly Daina was there, running down the dirt path as fast as her little legs could carry her. A foot from me she launched herself from the ground and catapulted up into my arms. I laughed at the same time as hot tears filled my eyes, struggling to blink them away. Daina wound her hands around my neck and planted half a dozen kisses on my cheek before burying her head into my shoulder. She was so light in my arms, feeling as if she weighed less than my five year old nephew, although she was seven. She clutched a bouquet of flowers that I knew were meant for me, but she had entirely forgotten them in her excitement. I swallowed back the lump in my throat and hugged her tightly as I situated her on my hip and our crowd continued to the courtyard.

There was Papa waiting for us. He had grown a beard since the last time I'd seen him, salt and pepper whiskers covering his cheeks and chin and melding with the familiar mustache. He walked to us, laughing in pleasure.

"Oh! Oh!" he cried as he hugged Caroline and then me. "Welcome!"

Behind him were Mama and housemothers Bubu and Madhu, and we greeted each other in embraces. Mama felt like a tiny frail creature and I held my arms around her lightly. Madhu beamed at me, her smile making her face even rounder than usual. Her hair had grown longer and was pulled back in a band at the nape of her neck. I was delighted to see my friend and thrilled that she was still there. Although our focus was the children, I knew that all the adults – Papa and Mama, the staff, the volunteers – were just as glad to see each other.

The pre-teen and older boys came trotting up. "Santosh!" I called as I spotted his face. I squeezed him tightly as he stood, typically, in his rigid stance with a blank face. All the boys crowded around while he remained nonchalant, almost ignoring my arrival. I knew him well enough by now to not let it hurt my feelings. I realized that any more fawning over him would embarrass him in the way most boys that age are embarrassed by such sentimental, babying displays of affection. I shook his hand, ruffled his hair and greeted the other boys.

Sure enough, Santosh remained by my side and gradually warmed up. Soon he had a smile on his face and was looking through my bag for the camera. I ventured to tell him I had missed him – in a low voice so no one else would hear the sappiness he was being subjected to – and then asked how he had been.

His face brightened. "I go to school!" he declared proudly, remembering his past troubles and our conversation about it. "Every day, I go to school."

The plastic chairs were pulled out and arranged in a circle, as they always were, under the big mango tree that hung over the courtyard. "Come!" Papa's voice boomed over the din. He took my wrist and steered me toward a chair with a hand planted on my back. "Come, you sit," he insisted. The second we were all seated the chai tea appeared. Madhu held a tray of tiny, steaming cups in front of me and in that moment, I felt everything I loved about this place converge together inside me. I breathed in all that I had missed.

The smell of the chai, its cardamom, ginger and cinnamon drifting up to my nose, the sound of bare feet slapping against the ground as children ran. The soft breeze that whispered through the trees and caressed my skin while the fading sun bathed everything in an orange and pink light. The colorful painted elephants that seemed to watch over us from their places on the surrounding walls. The vibrant blue and yellow and purple saris of the house mothers as they passed by and the bangles on their wrists that clinked melodically against each other while they worked. The occasional monkey above us in the trees, or a calf or dog that wandered into the courtyard before being shooed away by the staff. Most of all, the familiar faces around me that made me feel I had come home.

The very existence of these children had forever altered both the person I was and my view of the world. In some ways I felt more familiar to myself here, like I was now the person I had been brought to India to become. I had arrived, that first time two years before, not really knowing what to expect. I had not come to India to change anything about it; instead, the country and its people had worked a transformational change in me. They had allowed me into the real heart of the place and by doing so spared me from viewing it with the eyes of an outsider.

India's rawness of life strips away the unnecessary – distractions, superficial attachments, trivial worries. Without this safety net life becomes fundamental, only the essentials of being, and causes you to be fully present in your own existence. You become lost, in order to find. Revealed are not only the blemishes and horrors of the country that might be recoiled from – child beggars, lepers, humans sleeping in the street like animals – but also revealed are the blemishes within ourselves, stains on our own souls. At home, these things are hidden neatly away as much as it is possible to do so, our horrors and despairs swept neatly behind an outer façade that presents a more acceptable picture. Though my own society harbors many of the same ills – panhandlers and the homeless and economic disparity – here there is no pretense about it.

In India, everything is in full view; nothing is hidden. If I am repulsed without feeling compassion, my character is lessened. If I am aghast without recognizing the inequitable and appalling facets of my own culture, it is a reflection of my own true self. If I run away because it is selfishly easier than facing reality, it leaves a gaping hole in my connection to the human condition, that cloth of which we are all a part. India shows us where our suffering lies, and in this way becomes more than anything else a teacher, if only we are open to learn from her.

There is a fundamental difference between a tourist and a traveler. Rolf Potts, a travel writer and friend, summed it up perfectly when he wrote, "Tourists leave home to escape the world, while travelers leave home to experience it." People may come to India and view it with their own lens of bias, expectations and habits firmly in place. From there, it's far too easy to be shuttled from place to place, safely cocooned in cars and five-star hotels from which they gaze out at the spectacle passing before them. They dutifully traipse around the Taj Mahal and Varanasi with their video cameras before returning home, perhaps with the feeling that they've missed something essential.

But they never really saw India. Without stepping foot off the carefully guided path, they missed the opportunity to meet any Indians besides those workers who served them; never had tea in an Indian home or learned of the lives behind the faces. They were completely shielded from the real India; and for this I mourn, because they have been denied its very soul.

The beauty that lies in such a journey is the fact that everything is new and unfamiliar – the people, the language, the culture, the traditions, the food. To truly experience its joys requires fresh eyes and an immersion in this new world. India simply cannot be approached with anything but fully open arms and a willing heart. And it will embrace you in return with an exhilarated spirit, splendor and enchantment, nonstop vitality, amazing

people and their daily parade of life – struggles, joys and
triumphs – that passes by every moment.

I was lucky enough to have been given this incredible
treasure by these children and the people of India.

* * *

There was a tap on my shoulder and I looked around
just in time to see Caroline's Sibani duck down behind my
chair. "Who's there?" I asked in surprise, playing along
even as her muffled giggles were quite clear. I turned back
to face front and, soon enough, there was another tap,
another duck and round of satisfied snickering.

Sukru approached with a tube of henna and held her
hand out for mine. She had painted and hennaed me at least
once on every visit, and now led me into the girls' dorm and
began work on my hands. Sibani followed with Daina and
they began dancing, full of the natural exuberance that
possessed them both. Sisters Mami and Sumi sat nearby,
hesitantly eager for someone to notice them. I blew them
kisses with my free hand and they beamed, turning to each
other to share their delight in an almost twin-like way.

Sukru worked on her intricate henna design, bent over
my palm with a serious face. She was a contemplative teen,
cupping her mouth with a hand when she smiled as if
embarrassed to be caught in the act. She was a girl who
liked to have her world in order, neatly arranged just so.
She would line the younger children up for meals or
activities the way she lined her powders and brushes and
schoolbooks along the lid of her foot locker, moving each

item precisely until satisfied it was in its optimum balanced place. At seventeen, adulthood and the prospect of marriage or work looming, perhaps she felt she could control her future if she could exercise what little control she had over her current life.

* * *

Later that evening as we waited in the courtyard for the dinner bell, Caroline led the kids in a rousing bout of "Head, Shoulders, Knees and Toes." As one a huge group of people touched their shoulders and then bent down to touch knees and toes. The refrain grew faster and faster until the singing game collapsed into a mass of unsynchronized moves and peals of laughter. In the midst of it, however, Santosh and Tapas stood and executed it perfectly even when it became so fast that Caroline couldn't keep up with leading it. Santosh and Tapas continued, gazing at each other in a challenge as to who would falter first. Tapas smiled while Santosh's face was sober and intent, as if winning were the most important thing in the world at that moment.

Caroline flopped down beside me and caught her breath. "It's amazing how things have changed for these kids," she mused, looking around her. I couldn't help thinking how much they had changed for her, too. In seven years she had gone from a high-income, high-powered executive to a tireless advocate for these children. Her income had dropped from six figures to about thirty thousand dollars a year, and she had depleted her entire savings to get the Miracle Foundation off the ground.

But just as obvious to me was the fact that she had found her missing piece. For an unmarried woman with no children of her own, she had become "mother" to two hundred and fifty kids on the other side of the world. Over the years I had known her, I heard many people express open curiosity and amazement that she had taken on such work, in a foreign country at that, often the hardest parts of India. Tiny rural towns in small pockets of the earth. No fancy hotels, no restaurants, no luxuries. Far from it – we were all constantly dirty, sweaty, exhausted and hungry.

Here the messiness of life was living and dying in the streets, on full view right before our eyes. And it was most definitely overwhelming, even shocking. We were surrounded by some of the most heart-breaking circumstances, witnessing suffering so often that, quite honestly, I sometimes wanted to put my hands over my eyes and turn away. Surely Caroline had felt the same way countless times. How could she stand to hear such stories, deal with such poverty and deprivation day in and day out without being wasted emotionally? I posed to her the question I had so often heard others muse about.

"How do you do it?" I asked. "Isn't it ever just too difficult?"

She contemplated the question. "You know, for me being here is always temporary. I get to go back home, to indoor plumbing and electricity, my comfortable bed, restaurants and grocery stores full of any kind of food I want to buy." For those we left behind, the hardships we merely glimpsed continued. For them, it was everyday reality.

"So no, it isn't difficult," Caroline concluded; but I could see that she was agitated and encouraged her to expound further.

"I do get frustrated when people say that's just the way it is," she admitted. "Excuse me, but that's bullshit. Separate water fountains for blacks and whites back home was 'just the way it was' for a long time, but fortunately a lot of people refused to accept that. The time for philanthropy is now. But we shouldn't come here thinking we will teach these people something, or take over and tell them how to do things. I've been fortunate enough to work with some brilliant people here, and if we're smart we come here to listen and to learn. Together let's put our feet down and stop allowing children to starve."

On impulse, I asked if she had any regrets about what she had given up to do this.

"My income sure doesn't support the same wardrobe," she joked. But the smile quickly faded. "Sure, there's a comfort level in knowing you have the things money can buy – but I have everything money can't buy. I have peace. I know what I'm supposed to be doing with my life, and I'm on my purpose. I feel so fortunate to have found that."

Her eyes on me were strong and unwavering, and in her gaze I saw that although she had begun her journey thinking to help these children, she had discovered somewhere along the way that it was she who had been rescued by them. "I'm the lucky one, because I get to be the giver. In the end, that's how we get blessed," she said. "So many people go their whole lives without ever finding their purpose."

* * *

On my last night in India I sat in my hotel room in complete silence, with no distractions. No television or music, no reading, no open window for car horns and voices and clanging temple bells to drift up to me. I simply sat and contemplated everything I had seen and heard and done. As the sky grew deeper outside the window, dusky purple and orange darkening until there was nothing but black in the rectangle of glass, I took out each memory one at a time like a gem from a black velvet bag, turning it over until I felt ready to look at the next one. I thought about the laughter and despair; the nobility I had witnessed in the midst of wretched circumstances; those I loved so that the thought of leaving them again was a sharp needle piercing me; and those I had met for only moments, yet who felt bonded to me by the sorrows they had shared.

I was merely the scribe, one who listened to the stories each had to tell and then attempted to convey those powerful voices to others. I was indebted to everyone I had met who helped me along the journey, awed by the lives that had been laid bare. Although at times I wanted to look away from some exposed grief, I never quite could because even if I did the suffering remained. The poverty and hardships are still there whether we choose to see them or not. They do not go away simply because we decide that to be a witness to them, to say I care about your story, is too difficult for us.

In those darker moments I wondered when these children will matter to enough people. Few stop to see them, to care about them – fewer yet even think about them. How can we pretend they don't exist? I have cried many times for those I have known: Santosh and Daina, Yesu Babu working for his grandmother and HIV-positive brother, little Anantha in the frilly yellow dress at Little Hearts home, Rashid struggling to write with his mouth and amputated arms – and for the millions more out there I've never met. I have wept hot tears of utter helplessness at being unable to do enough to assuage their losses; wounded by the unfairness, by the abundance I see all around me every day against the stark comparison to their world. It is impossible for me to reconcile the co-existence of extravagant material prosperity and abject poverty in our world.

But I have also shed tears of gratitude over the unconditional love they have shown me, simple joy shared even in the face of so little. From suffering, whether our own or that which we are a witness to, something opens up inside and in that opening we can be either consumed or liberated. Its wound leaves a scar – but also a message, something that becomes a part of me to learn from when I'm ready, and later draw on when I need strength. If true happiness does, indeed, lie in the sharing of love then these young people surely possess some innate joy beyond measure, for being with them I experienced a simple contentment which has seeped into my core and made its permanent home there. Children who inhabit not even a corner of the world, pushed to its very margins.

Yet their impact has not only been felt, but resonated, among hundreds if not thousands of others besides myself. The social workers, volunteers, donors, doctors, teachers I have met – countless people whose lives have been touched and changed by these children. Attitudes of cynicism or despair can sometimes prevail when confronted by the enormity of such challenges; that it is such a monumental task as to be insurmountable, a problem without solutions. But the truth I have found over visits to dozens of organizations and hours upon hours of interviews, is that all over India – and beyond its borders – people are striving tirelessly every day in initiatives and programs which, if scaled up and coordinated and funded in full measure throughout the country, would have an immeasurable impact on such vulnerable children's lives and futures. Through this alone, the meaning of their being holds more than the greatest among us could ever hope to achieve. They have embodied hope, love, faith and charity in a way that is rarely found upon this earth – without even knowing it.

* * *

Spring 2008

One year later, life had continued for the world, as well as in the smaller worlds of these children. I had sent a donation to assist Yesu Babu, working to support his HIV-positive brother and elderly grandmother in the Vambay slum outside Vijayawada. I learned from Keerthi Bollineni of the VMM social organization that it would take only five hundred dollars to pay for the family's home, food and other living expenses for an entire year, which would allow Yesu to stop working and go to school. His younger brother, Venugopal, was still receiving medical treatment and going to school as well.

Anantha of the frilly yellow dress had been at the Little Hearts home in Andhra Pradesh, being cared for by C.P. Kumar and his family, until January of 2008. That's when her grandmother came to get her for a visit from their home village three hundred-fifty kilometers away. Days after she left with her granddaughter, C.P. received a phone call saying that she was bringing Anantha back to Little Hearts. But by June 2008 the little girl had still not come back. C.P. told me, "I am expecting Anantha will be back this month after school re-opens on the twelfth."

In the year since I had visited, C.P.'s work was expanding at a rapid rate. He had increased his services to HIV-positive women and children in the surrounding areas, establishing satellite homes for children and training and micro-finance programs for poor rural women.

Sahiful and the other boy filmmakers at CCD's

Muktaneer Home in Calcutta had recently been featured in another film festival for their latest movie, made entirely by the children who were former laborers. *We See* was featured in the Culture Unplugged Studios 2008 Film Festival, and was the seventh most popular movie out of more than two hundred-ninety films entered. For his work of giving the boys cameras and filmmaking skills, as well as his incredible undertaking to free hundreds of children from trafficking and labor, CCD secretary Swapan Mukherjee was awarded the Real Heroes Award in April 2008. The award is meant to honor the unsung heroes of India; ordinary people who have done extraordinary things for the well being of others in the country.

No one knew what had happened to Rashid, the boy whose arms had been amputated and lived mostly in the Kurla train station in Mumbai. Oasis India had closed down the program that provided clothing, food, play and learning activities for the railway boys, in favor of a more preventative approach. Communications Manager Divya Kottadiel wrote me in an email, "The Ashadeep centre has closed down and we have another project in place which is the South Asia Centre for Missing & Exploited Persons to trace missing children, many of whom are brought through Kurla station."

My sponsored angel, Daina, was doing well in Papa's orphanage in Northeast India. She had recuperated from a bad cold caught over the winter; I had been sent a photo of her in December in which she looked pale and wan. But by March 2008 she was rosy-cheeked and full of energy again.

Caroline visited that month and reported back to me that the little girl was thriving, although she did notice that as Daina grew bigger she was starting to become rather bossy with the younger children.

Unfortunately, news about Santosh wasn't so reassuring. He was no longer at the ashram, having been taken away by his father, and was now living in the village. Several other boys of about the same age, twelve to fifteen years old, had also left to go back to their village. This was all the information I had, and it was little to go on. I couldn't help but have conflicting feelings and worry about his situation. On the one hand, my deepest wish for all these children was to have their own homes and families to live with. If circumstances had changed for Santosh's father and he was now able to care for his son, I would be very happy for the boy I had grown to know and love over the past several years.

But in the back of my mind was the thought that Santosh and the other boys who had left were at an age when they could be put to work. If this was the driving force behind Santosh being taken back, his present situation might be worse than at the orphanage. If he was working, it was almost certain he was no longer in school. I vowed to return to India soon and find him before he risked becoming lost forever. If I could help support his family so that Santosh could live at home and still attend school, I wanted to do that. But for now, I did not know anything more specific. An uneasy dread sat heavily in the bottom of my heart.

And at the same time, new children without homes or care were arriving daily. At Manjeet's orphanage in Rourkela a girl of about twelve, Santosh's age, was brought to the gates by a police officer. It was the end of the second day of Caroline's visit with a group of volunteers, and they were packed up and waiting for the cars to drive them back to the hotel when the officer knocked at the front gate.

The policewoman entered, pulling along behind her a filthy girl dressed in what could only be called rags. She was clearly terrified. Yet, at the same time, her eyes were blank. As her story, or what little was known of it, was revealed to house mother Joyti, it seemed clear the girl had seen and lived too much beyond her years. The officer explained that the child had been found living on the streets, and had been taken into the police station. After twenty-four hours, no relatives could be found and no one came forth to claim her. The girl either could not, or would not, reveal much about her past.

"There is nowhere else to take her but here," the officer told Joyti. And so the girl was brought in. Over the next several days she mostly kept to herself, away from the other children and silent. She was given new clothes to wear, but would consistently sneak off and return wearing her old filthy garments which hung in tatters around her. Joyti allowed her to do so, not knowing exactly the reason why. Perhaps she felt more secure in her own clothing, or it was the fact that they were the only things in the world that belonged to her. It was also possible that she didn't feel she deserved the new clothes, questioning the motives behind what she was being given and wondered at what moment it would all be taken away.

I had hopes for this girl, because she was now in the care of Manjeet, Joyti and the other housemothers. I had seen countless other children just like her. Months later they were laughing and thriving, happy and healthy, well-adjusted kids. The natural resiliency of children was one of the greatest factors in their favor, and as long as they were found by caring adults and taken into programs that could give them the basic rights they were entitled to – a home, food, clean water, medical care and an education – miracles could happen, and did every day.

* * *

In a 1967 address in New York City, Dr. Martin Luther King, Jr. said, "True compassion is more than flinging a coin to a beggar. It comes to see that an edifice which produces beggars needs restructuring. A true revolution of values will soon look uneasily on the glaring contrast of poverty and wealth. With righteous indignation, it will look across the seas and see individual capitalists of the West investing huge sums of money in Asia, Africa, and South America, only to take the profits out with no concern for the social betterment of the countries, and say, 'This is not just.'"

In this, one of the most important speeches in American history, Dr. King was speaking about the Vietnam War; yet his words resonate just as clearly with me today as I think about India and her twenty-five million parentless children. Dr. King went on to charge, "The Western arrogance of

feeling that it has everything to teach others and nothing to
learn from them is not just. This call for a worldwide
fellowship that lifts neighborly concern beyond one's tribe,
race, class, and nation is in reality a call for an all-embracing
and unconditional love for all mankind. We are confronted
with the fierce urgency of now. In this unfolding
conundrum of life and history, there is such a thing as being
too late."[cliv]

I desperately hope we will not be too late for these
children. And so I wait for the day when we realize it is up
to us. Every one of us. No one is exempt, everyone has their
part to play. We owe it to them and to the world. And
ultimately, we owe it to ourselves.

At home I meditate sometimes to a CD recording of
"my kids" in Orissa singing their prayer songs. Mostly I
close my eyes, trying to follow the Buddhist way of clearing
my mind of all the clutter, the constant jumble and noise of
a thousand trivial things that clamor for my attention. In
that empty space, I let the small sweet voices fill me as they
do in India, trying to transport myself back to that time and
place.

But occasionally my eyes open and when they do, they
fall on a wall hanging I bought in Udaipur, made up of the
scraps from dozens of saris. I gaze at the handmade
patchwork, its many colors and patterns so carefully
stitched together by the craftsman. Each small individual
piece of material, before it was sewn into the finished
product, is fragile and insignificant. It is not anything except
a torn scrap of cloth, beautiful but delicate, easily ripped or

lost. Yet, when it is stitched together strongly to the next tiny piece, and then the next, suddenly the pattern of the whole begins to take form. The finished patchwork, all these scraps of what was once discarded, together are strong. Together they make something. They have a purpose - to cover a bed, to keep a child warm or, as in my house, to simply be beautiful.

And so it is with these children of India – the orphans, the street kids, the world's forgotten throwaways. They may be fragile and easily lost on their own, but held together with the thread of those who care – the organizations and people who labor as lovingly and painstakingly as this artisan to make sure the children aren't discarded but are held together and cherished – then they can be seen as a whole, strong and vibrant; and above all they are, simply, beautiful.

---

cliv King, Dr. Martin Luther Jr. "Beyond Vietnam," April 4, 1967. http://www.africanamericans.com/MLKjrBeyondVietnam.htm.

Caroline Boudreaux greets the Miracle Foundation children in Orissa

Damodar "Papa" Sahoo hugs Meena and Santa

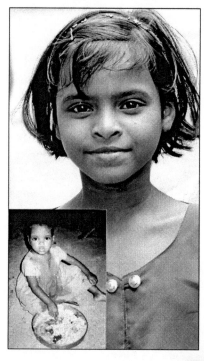

Sibani in 2009, and on the fateful night she and Caroline met in 2000

Photo courtesy of Svetlana Forlova.

Dr. Manjeet Pardesi, Director of Miracle Foundation operations in India

Sisters Mami (left) and Sumi (center), with Seale's sponsored child Daina

Life in the shanty village by the river, outside Cuttack, Orissa

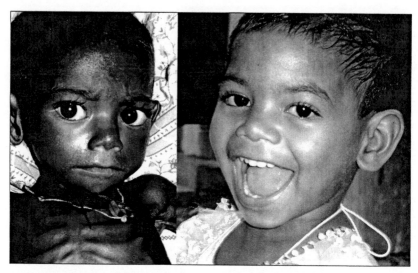

Sumitra, who arrived in the middle of the night in 2006, shown again in 2007

Little Hearts founder C.P. Kumar (top center) with the children of the home. Photo courtesy of Stewart Botting

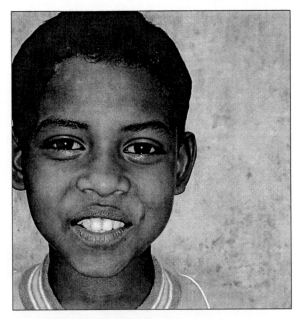

Amir, the boy who just wants to be a father when he grows up

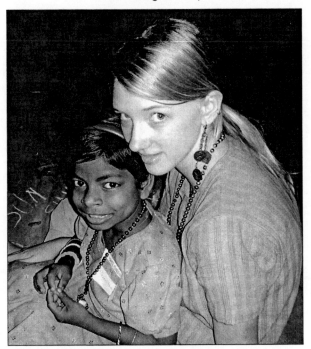

Seale's daughter, Chandler, with Sumi in 2006

Santosh, left, and friend at the Miracle Foundation home in Orissa

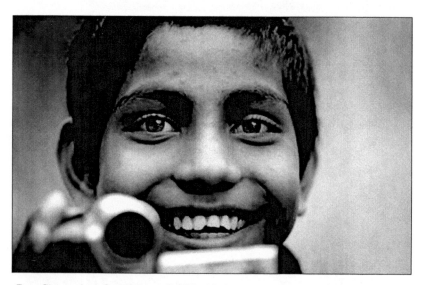

Boy filmmaker Sahiful, at CCD's Muktaneer Home in Calcutta

A child in the Dharavi slum of Mumbai; photo courtesy of Deepa Krishnan

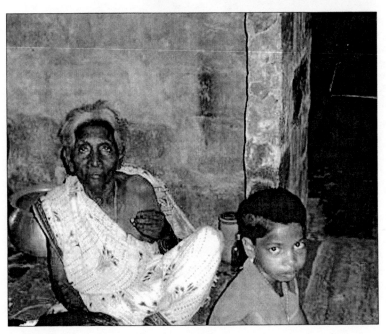

Ramulamma and her grandson Krishna in Vambay Colony, Andhra Pradesh

Anjana, the girl brought by police to the Rourkela home in
March 2008

Author Shelley Seale

"Our lives begin to end the day we become silent
about things that matter."

--Dr. Martin Luther King, Jr.

Resources

If you would like to make an impact for these children and become involved in upholding their rights, there are many different ways for you to do so – from volunteering or donating money, to doing something as quick and easy as signing a petition or sending an email to your representative. Below is a list of resources to get you started. You may also visit the Weight of Silence blog for regular updates and more ways to help: http://weightofsilence.wordpress.com.

Please write to your senators and representatives, urging them to support United Nations' and global efforts at ended child labor, trafficking and slavery: http://www.usa.gov/Contact/Elected.shtml

Organizations the author has personally visited and profiled in this book:

The Miracle Foundation: www.miraclefoundation.org Caroline Boudreaux, Phone: +1 512 329-8635, Email: info@miraclefoundation.org

Little HEARTS Orphanage: www.globalgiving.com/pr/1200/proj1131d.html C.P. Kumar, Phone: +91 99 4920 2919, Email: heartsindia@yahoo.com

Divine Childrens Home: www.divinechildrens.com Alice Thomas, Phone: +91 47 1325 5273, Email: dchtvm@rediffmail.com

CHES Community Health Education Society: www.pbase.com/maciekda/ches_aids

Dr. P. Manorama, Phone: +91 44 2473 1283, Email: pmanorama@yahoo.com

Vasavya Mahila Mandali: www.vasavya.com
Keerthi Bollineni, Phone: +91 86 6247 0966, Email: vasavya@vasavya.com

CCD – Centre of Communication and Development: www.ccdftcindia.org
Swapan Mukherjee, Phone: +91 33 2537 4660, Email: ccdftc1@cal2.vsnl.net.in

Oasis India: www.oasisindia.org
Divya Kottadiel, Phone: +91 22 4048 5400, Email: transformation@oasisindia.org

Akanksha: www.akanksha.org
Tina Vajpeyi, Phone: +91 22 2370 0253, Email: website@akanksha.org
Heroes Project: www.heroesprojectindia.org
Swati Mohapatra ,Phone: +91 22 2519 4713, Email: swatim@heroesprojectindia.org

Salaam Baalak Trust: www.salaamstreetkids.org
Kalyani Nair, Phone: +91 22 2374 4148, Email: info@salaamstreetkids.org

The Naz Foundation: www.nazindia.org
Anjali Gopalan, Phone: +91 11 2691 0499, Email: naz@nazindia.org

Pratham Mumbai Outreach: www.pratham.org
Farida Lambay, Phone: +91 22 2281 9561, Email: mumbai@pratham.org

World Vision India: www.WorldVisionIndia.org
Jayanth Vincent, Phone: +91 44 2480 7070, Email: indiasponsors@wvi.org

Websites that Work for Children's Rights Worldwide:

One Campaign to End Poverty: www.one.org

Child Slavery Action Blog: www.stopchildslavery.com

Global March Against Child Labor: www.globalmarch.org

Namaste India Children's Fund: www.NICFund.org

The Better World Shopping Guide:
www.betterworldshopper.com

Child Haven International: www.childhaven.ca

Volunteer Opportunities:

Miracle Foundation's volunteer travel website:
http://miraclefoundation.org/index.php?pid=198

Global Volunteers: www.globalvolunteers.org

Global Vision International: www.gvi.co.uk

Voluntourism.org: www.voluntourism.org

Stuff Your Rucksack: www.stuffyourrucksack.com